# Though the Winds Blow

# Though the Winds Blow

A Daily Guide to Successful Living

BY ROBERT H. PIERSON

SOUTHERN PUBLISHING ASSOCIATION
NASHVILLE, TENNESSEE

# Foreword

Winds are blowing over this aging earth—winds of storm, winds of change, winds of strife. Over emerging Africa, exploding Vietnam, in troubled Europe, in the tortured inner cities of America, they shriek and howl in fiendish glee, leaving death and destruction in their wake. What is their significance? Is the voice of God in the howling blast? Is He seeking to speak to us earthbound mortals through the events of our day? He is!

Though the winds blow, though we live in an age of strife and commotion, there is refuge, there is help and hope—even happiness—for all who long to escape the troubled physical and political elements threatening to engulf them. The intent of this book is not to ignore the storm, but to point out a refuge from it—to help guide one through the tempest to the quiet haven of peace, here and hereafter.

May God bless you as you read, and may you find that help and hope and happiness—THOUGH THE WINDS BLOW.

ROBERT H. PIERSON

# Acknowledgments

In addition to the King James Version of the Bible, the following versions have been quoted:

Revised Standard Version.

Rotherham's Translation.

Amplified New Testament.

The New Testament in Modern English. Copyright, J. B. Phillips, 1958. Used by permission of The Macmillan Company.

The New English Bible, New Testament. Copyright, The Delegates of the Oxford University Press and The Syndics of the Cambridge University Press, 1961. Reprinted by permission.

The Bible: A New Translation by James Moffatt. Copyright, 1954. Used by permission of Harper and Row, Publishers, Inc.

# Contents

# SECTION I

# There Are Thousands Like Him

"I've just killed Bill Fridlin!" an agitated voice announced over the telephone to a friend of mine. "The police are outside, but they'll never take me alive. I have a gun. I'm going to end it all. I tell you, I'm going to end it all. There's nothing to live for!"

Phil Terry nearly dropped his phone. "But, Fred, you can't do it! What's happened? Tell me!" My shocked friend stalled for time, for words.

"There's no use living, Mr. Terry," the distraught youth continued. "I just can't take it any longer. Everything's gone wrong! I'm going to kill myself!" Fred Howman's words trailed off disconsolately.

"Wait a minute, Fred! Wait a minute! Let's talk this over. There must be some way out." Phil's brain worked desperately. After all, what does one say to an employee who has gone berserk and at that very moment is holding a gun to his head, threatening to pull the trigger before the law shoots its way in? "You can't do it, Fred. There's your family. There's Mary and the kids!"

"They don't care!" Fred's voice quavered. "They don't care. They'll be better off without me. I'm going to do it, I tell you!"

13

Phil knew there had been problems—real problems—in the young man's home. He knew about the debts and other difficulties. Faintly he recalled that there had been bad feelings between Fred and Bill—but this—no, it couldn't be! It wasn't true. Fred wouldn't settle things this way.

Through the receiver Phil could hear shouts in the background. The insistent voices of the police demanded that Fred let them in. Fred was desperate. Sketchily he sobbed out the brief, sad story. It ended with another threat to do away with himself.

"Don't do it, Fred! For God's sake, don't do it! There's some way out, but not that way!" Phil prayed as he pleaded, "Put down that gun! Give yourself up. I'll be right over and see what I can do to help you. Promise me, Fred, you won't do it. Let the police in. Talk to them. I'll be right over!"

Fred gave a reluctant half promise and clicked the phone down.

A few days later a confused, remorseful Fred Howman faced a charge of homicide in the county court.

Multiplied thousands of Fred Howmans crowd the world today—discouraged, frustrated, fed-up human beings living with confused minds and jaded nerves, existing on aspirin and coffee breaks, apparently with no hope, no reason for "going on." They live in a generation of discontent and lawlessness, of escapism and moral bankruptcy—a time when an evil sickness of mind and soul grips far too many of the human race.

What to do? Is there no help, no hope, no way out?

There is help! There is hope! There *is* a way out. Even Fred Howmans are not hopeless. And, what may be far more pertinent—help exists for you, for me, in those moments of fear and discouragement when things look dark ahead.

"Thou shalt be secure, because there is hope." Job 11:18.

*Monday*

# But There Is Hope

"A direct hit!" crackled the loudspeaker. "Every man to his station. Use all emergency measures!" But the ocean poured through the mangled hull with a deafening roar. Those who could, escaped overboard. An explosion, a shudder, and the proud warship slid beneath the waves. For a moment silence covered the sea. Then the fight for survival continued. A few swam toward the distant shore, some clung to floating debris, and others found life rafts.

In a short time help came and with it rescue equipment. The divers probed the depths and found more men—some dead, some alive. Then from deep in the vessel the workmen heard a strange tapping. They listened. It sounded like someone trying to attract their attention. Yes, it was! It was the Morse code. Carefully they spelled out the words the unknown man below was trying to get through—"I-S T-H-E-R-E H-O-P-E?" Hope—that was what the man trapped in the terrifying silence below wanted more than anything else in the world—*hope*—the hope of a way out!

Hope—a way out of its present baffling impasse —is what our confused, chaotic, lost world needs. Is such hope to be found? If so, where?

Paul tells us that we "might grasp the hope that he holds out to us. This hope, . . . the utterly reliable anchor for our souls." (Hebrews 6:18, Phillips.) Paul also reveals the source of such hope. "Yes, Christ *in you* bringing with him the hope of all the glorious things to come." Colossians 1:27, Phillips.

There is hope. Through the shadows and the tears we can still trace the form of the only One who gives us hope for today, tomorrow, and forever. It is for us to decide that even though things go wrong, we can rise above them.

Listen to the certainty of Peter's hope: "So brace up your minds, and, as men who know what they are doing, rest the full weight of your hopes on the grace

"Is there hope?" the sailor signaled on the bulkhead.

that will be yours when Jesus Christ reveals himself." 1 Peter 1:13, Phillips.

Pause and study Watts's great picture called "Hope." A woman stands alone upon the round earth—blindfolded. In her hands she holds a harp on which all but one string have snapped. Above her, in the semidarkness, one little star shines. She is playing her harp, still making music.

This is hope. We may have lost almost everything in life, but we can go on making the most of what is left.

We may have lost money—money perhaps saved with great care and self-denial for the expenses of old age. It has been swept away. What of it? It was nothing but money. Some may have lost health. No greater disaster can come upon anyone. Yet many in the world have in spite of burdened, sick bodies played rich and noble music upon the strings that are left. Money, health, happiness, may seem to have fled, but some strings are still left, one star still gleams in the darkened sky.

An author who met and conquered many difficulties writes, "None need abandon themselves to discouragement and despair. Satan may come to you with the cruel suggestion, 'Yours is a hopeless case. You are irredeemable.' But there is hope for you in Christ. God does not bid us overcome in our own strength. He asks us to come close to His side. Whatever difficulties we labor under, which weigh down soul and body, He waits to make us free."—*The Ministry of Healing,* p. 249.

Many times angels work through human beings to bring hope, joy, and peace to the sick or suffering. Those who receive such help are doubly blessed. Many find health again—the uncertain step becomes buoyant, dull eyes sparkle, despondency becomes joy, complaining turns to gratitude. The hopeless one finds hope.

"May the God of hope fill *you* with joy and peace in your faith, that by the power of the Holy Spirit, your whole life and outlook may be radiant with hope." Romans 15:13, Phillips.

Hope? Yes! For today—and for tomorrow.

*Tuesday*

# Joy Inside Out

Some years ago in the Orange Free State, South Africa, I met Mrs. Ellen Dippenaar. She was radiant with an inward joy, everything about her diffusing happiness. But Mrs. Dippenaar was blind and confined to a wheelchair, with hands badly disfigured.

Years earlier Ellen Dippenaar had contracted leprosy. During the time she spent in the leprosarium heartaches came in Joblike succession: her only son died of polio, her husband succumbed to cancer, a sister was killed in an automobile crash.

And one day while putting drops in Ellen's eyes, the nurse made a horrible mistake—the "eye drops" turned out to be carbolic acid, and Ellen's sight was destroyed. A short time later gangrene necessitated the amputation of one leg. During the first fifty-five years of her life Mrs. Dippenaar had had fifty-six operations, and it seemed incredible that one person could have had so much heartache, so many calamities, in one lifetime.

What would you expect a woman who had experienced so many tragedies to talk about? Her misfortunes? Her bad luck? The unfairness of it all? Not Ellen Dippenaar. Ellen talked of her blessings, of the goodness of God, of all He had done for her. It was no sham, no cover-up. Ellen's radiant face confirmed every word she spoke.

Mrs. Dippenaar had learned the source of joy just as another Christian named Bill Kinsey had discovered it.

"I think Bill Kinsey goes to heaven every night," Betty, a small girl, exclaimed.

"Why do you say that?" her mother asked.

"Mamma, Mr. Kinsey must go to heaven every night, 'cause he's so happy every day!"

Bill Kinsey had his own explanation for the joy he knew. "Joy," Bill said, "is the flag that flies from the castle of the heart when the King is in residence there."

When the King is "in residence" in any heart—Ellen Dippenaar's, Bill Kinsey's, yours, or mine—joy will be there, too. True Christianity is not all pie in the sky, not all heaven in the hereafter. The Apostle Peter tells us that in following Jesus, "even now he brings you a joy that words cannot express and which has in it a hint of the glories of Heaven." (1 Peter 1:8, Phillips.) Paul confirms the assurance of his fellow apostle: "This doesn't mean, of course, that we have only a hope of future joys—we can be full of joy here and now even in our trials and troubles." Romans 5:3, Phillips.

Christ came among men to bring joy. The angel's exultant announcement of His birth is filled with joy: "Fear not: for, behold, I bring you good tidings of great joy, which shall be to all people. For unto you is born this day in the city of David a Saviour, which is Christ the Lord." Luke 2:10, 11.

Ellen G. White describes it this way: "The Prince of heaven was among His people. The greatest gift of God had been given to the world. Joy to the poor; for Christ had come to make them heirs of His kingdom. Joy to the rich; for He would teach them how to secure eternal riches. Joy to the ignorant; He would make them wise unto salvation. Joy to the learned; He would open to them deeper mysteries than they had ever fathomed; truths that had been hidden from the foundation of the world would be opened to men by the Saviour's mission."—*The Desire of Ages,* p. 277.

The Scriptures say much about joy in the hearts of men who knew God: "Therefore with joy shall ye draw water out of the wells of salvation." Isaiah 12:3. "In thy presence is fulness of joy." Psalm 16:11. "Her saints shall shout aloud for joy." Psalm 132:16. "I will greatly rejoice in the Lord, my soul shall be joyful in my God." Isaiah 61:10. "Ye rejoice with joy unspeakable and full of glory." 1 Peter 1:8.

Someone has described the prescription of joy in the following acrostic:

J    esus—first

O    thers—second

Y    ou—third

Serving Christ is not a grudging obedience. It is a *joy!* It is an experience of love and joy to live in harmony with our Saviour and Friend. The Christian connects himself with the greatest source of joy in the entire universe. Christ Himself is the principle of eternal joy and happiness.

*Wednesday*

# Where Happiness Is

"I wouldn't want to continue to live if I knew I would never be happy." The thoughtful young man seated in front of me meant every word he said.

How about you? If you knew that happiness would never be yours, would you want to live? Every human heart craves happiness. Every individual has spent some of his life, his energy, his wealth, in search of this ofttimes illusive experience.

In your search for happiness you may be successful, but happiness may not be exactly where you expect to find it.

First, let's close those dead-end doors.

Some time ago I read a newspaper story about a fabulously wealthy European couple. The man lavished all sorts of gifts upon his wife. He gave her a yacht valued at several million dollars. When she went shopping for trinkets in a foreign port, a fleet of limousines followed her from shop to shop. The bill for one such shopping spree came to over $50,-000. Anything money could buy was hers.

After thirteen years of marriage, the wife of this wealthy man said, "His great wealth has not brought me happiness with him, nor has it brought him happiness with me."

Centuries ago one of the wealthiest and wisest men who ever lived wrote, "He that trusteth in his riches shall fall." "Riches profit not in the day of wrath." Proverbs 11:28, 4. Wealth will purchase almost anything—but happiness.

King Solomon looked for happiness where many today search for it: in the pleasures this world has to offer—wine, women, and song. Using the resources of the Hebrew nation, he searched deeply.

Solomon wrote, "I sought in mine heart to give myself unto wine . . . and to lay hold on folly." "I gathered me also silver and gold, and the peculiar treasure of kings: . . . I gat me men singers and women singers, and the delights of the sons of men, as musical instruments, and that of all sorts." Ecclesiastes 2:3, 8.

Of the drinking parties, the banquets, the dances, the concerts, and the lavish extravaganzas Solomon said, "Wine is a mocker, strong drink is raging: and whosoever is deceived thereby is not wise." "Who hath woe? who hath sorrow? who hath contentions? who hath babbling? who hath wounds without cause? who hath redness of eyes? They that tarry long at the wine; they that go to seek mixed wine." Proverbs 20:1; 23:29, 30.

Solomon also sought happiness in wisdom, in learning. "I gave my heart to seek and search out by wisdom concerning all things that are done under heaven," he exclaimed, and then added, "I have seen all the works that are done under the sun." Ecclesiastes 1:13, 14. He is described in the Scriptures this way: "He spake three thousand proverbs: and his songs were a thousand and five." "Solomon's wisdom excelled the wisdom of all the children of the east country, and all the wisdom of Egypt. For he was wiser than all men; . . . and his fame was in all nations round about." 1 Kings 4:32, 30, 31.

Let the wise man himself tell us whether this unparalleled wisdom and knowledge brought him true happiness: "In much wisdom is much grief: and he that increaseth knowledge increaseth sorrow." Then as a bit of a capsheaf of disillusionment he exclaims, "All is vanity and vexation of spirit." (Ecclesiastes 1:18, 14.)

In his more mature years Solomon *did* find happiness. He found it when his conscience was at rest and his heart right with God—when his life was in harmony with the will of his Maker. Solomon's prescription for true happiness is given in these words: "He that keepeth the law, happy is he." Proverbs 29:18.

This ancient king knew, as you and I should know, that someday our lives will be measured by God's Ten Commandment law (Ecclesiastes 12:13, 14), and that we can be truly happy only when our minds are free of offense toward God and man—

when we know that our sins are covered by the blood of Christ and that our future with Him is assured.

"Base your happiness on your hope in Christ," Paul says. (Romans 12:12, Phillips.) "Happy is that people, whose God is the Lord." Psalm 144:15.

This joy, this happiness, may be yours!

*Thursday*

# Though Disappointment Comes

Akbar had been working in a government office for three years, and he thought he was doing quite well in his work. But when time for promotion came, Akbar was left at his same old desk. Someone else in the department was moved up.

Disappointment changed to discouragement. Within a few days he was thoroughly depressed by a sense of failure. "Why has this happened to me? Is there something wrong with me?" he asked himself over and over again.

One evening after work Akbar walked across the dry rice paddy fields near his home to the dark irrigation canal flowing a short distance away.

"No use going on," he muttered. "No one appreciates me. I'll end it all in the canal. No one will miss me."

As the downcast youth shuffled along a narrow dike separating the paddy fields, kicking at small clods of dirt, he saw a piece of paper lying in the dust.

Akbar reached down and picked up a printed card.

"What Happens After Death?" he read. The card was an advertisement for a Christian Bible correspondence course. There were several other questions on the card which also aroused his curiosity.

After studying the striking contents of the card briefly, Akbar wavered in his decision to drown his troubles in the canal. He forgot some of his self-pity and decided to sign up for the correspondence course.

Soon the Bible lessons began coming regularly. Akbar discovered a new world of intellectual excitement which helped him forget his disappointment at not being promoted. The Bible course taught him that Someone did care for him and would help him solve his problems. He developed an entirely new attitude toward life and toward other people. Now he wanted to help others, as he stated in a letter to me one day.

As the Scriptures counsel, we are to "lay hold upon the hope set before us: which hope we have as an anchor of the soul, both sure and stedfast." (Hebrews 6:18, 19.)

*Friday*

# A New Light Burns

A tree crashed to earth with a fearful uproar. An agonized cry of pain was followed by a low moan, then silence.

Stunned, Bert Wilson lay pinned beneath a huge pine tree, his face showing the shock of sudden pain. Within seconds Duane Thurman was by his side struggling to free his friend.

Other workers were instantly on the scene and carefully pried the huge limb from the young man's crushed body. Tenderly they carried Bert, unconscious, to the nearby lumber camp.

On the rough bunk bed, awaiting the doctor's arrival, Bert slowly opened his eyes.

"I guess this is it, Duane!" Bert's lips moved slightly. "I'm not going to make it." He rested a few moments and the dry lips moved again. "Can't you help me, Duane?"

"The doctor will be here any minute now, Bert." Duane tried to reassure his friend. "Everything will be all right then."

"I'm afraid not," Bert said with labored effort. "What I need——" he paused and then continued, "is some help to die. Can't you say something about Him? Can't you help me? Can't you pray?" Bert looked up through anguished eyes. "I've been pretty tough—haven't had much time for God—but you're different, Duane. You ought to know! Can't you help me?" Bert whispered.

Duane was stunned. His face grew pale. Reared in a Christian home, his own father a minister, Duane had once planned on entering the ministry. But there had been skeptical classmates with seeds of doubt. Thinking himself intellectually superior, he had gradually lost his faith in God and given up his desire for the ministry. After writing defiantly to his father, Duane had fled to this job in the woods to get away from God, his father, and all the influences of the past. Now here he was—Bert's plaintive plea tugging at his mind, "Can't you help me?"

"Bert, I can't, I——" he couldn't say what he had felt in his heart the past year or so. He couldn't let Bert down that way. Something was happening in his own rebellious soul. Leaping to his feet, Duane rushed out into the forest. There, alone with God, he struggled with the anguished confrontation the events of the last hour had brought him. For five, ten minutes the distraught youth probed the depths of his proud heart. After all, God *did* matter! The Christ of his early years *was* real. There was only one choice for him to make, and there beneath the tall pines of the Northland Duane Thurman found his way back to God.

Hurrying back to the bunkhouse Duane saw Bert lying quietly, still waiting for the doctor to arrive. Falling on his knees by his stricken friend Duane had a new story to tell.

"Bert," he whispered, "I've been to God myself —and He's forgiven me. Now I can tell you the story!"

His body tortured with pain, Bert looked up hopefully. "Yes, Duane, tell me quickly. Tell me about Him!"

Simply, tenderly, so filled with hope, the story tumbled out. The love, the life, the cross—all for Bert. It came with a warmth only a renewed personal experience could have endowed it with. The words of John and Paul climaxed the good news: "But if we walk in the light, as he is in the light, we have fellowship one with another, and the blood of Jesus Christ his Son cleanseth us from all sin." 1 John 1:7. "But God commendeth his love toward us, in that, while we were yet sinners, Christ died for us." Romans 5:8.

A new light crept into Bert's eyes. "I see. For me there's hope! Thank God," he gasped.

There in the quiet sanctuary of the great North Woods two young men found God. One fell asleep in Christ a few minutes later; the other began a life of fruitful service for Christ his King, a service he had once rejected.

*Saturday*

# A More Abundant Life

Ellen G. White writes regarding the work of Christ, "In every city, every town, every village, through which He passed, He laid His hands upon the afflicted ones and healed them. . . . During His ministry, Jesus devoted more time to healing the sick than to preaching."—*The Ministry of Healing,* pp. 18, 19.

For some, blind from birth, the face of the Master appeared like a vision of beauty out of an abyss of night. For deaf men the sweet voice of Jesus was the first sound to pierce the awful silence. Dumb men shouted His praise. Lepers felt the cleansing power of healing. Paralytics felt strength coursing through unfeeling limbs. Truly the Saviour came that men "might have life, and that they might have it more abundantly." (John 10:10.)

What Jesus did yesterday He is able to do today. He is "the same yesterday, and to day, and for ever." (Hebrews 13:8.) Of the needy sick the Word of God says, "The Eternal sustains him on his sick bed, and brings him back to health." Psalm 41:3, Moffatt. Our Great Physician says today, as He did to a despairing woman who had been ill for twelve years, "It is your faith that has healed you. Go home in peace, and be free from your trouble." Mark 5: 34, Phillips.

Jesus Christ is our all-sufficient Saviour. He not only frees us from sin, but He heals our sickness as well. Of this I am certain. The remainder of this book could well be devoted to the exhibits of His healing power.

Mrs. Frances Osborne was at death's door in the summer of 1962, in a Tennessee hospital. All hope seemed gone. She was anointed by her minister, who prayed earnestly for her recovery. A short time later I learned how wonderfully those prayers had been answered. Her mother wrote, "You will be glad to know that Frances is well and happy, teaching music again. She is a living example of God's healing power everywhere she goes."

In Pretoria, South Africa, I met John Roux, whom God had healed of leprosy.

In Windhoek, South-West Africa, the wife of a minister was not expected to live. A friend and I anointed her and prayed for her recovery. As we prayed, she fainted and remained unconscious for some time. Several years later I met her again, and she appeared to be well and strong. Her improvement began the day after the anointing service.

One day little Mark, an eight-month-old baby boy who lived in Lawrence, Kansas, was struck by a stray rifle bullet. The bullet hit about three quarters of an inch above the left ear and lodged near the surface behind the opposite ear. For days the child's life hung in the balance. The doctors feared that should he survive, his brain might be damaged. The pastor anointed the little fellow and pleaded with God for his recovery.

The heartfelt testimony of Mark's grateful parents is, "We believe that Mark was saved by direct answer to prayer and that we would not have our baby today had it not been for the intervention of God on his behalf."

So the story could go on and on—a glorious paean of praise and power! The song states, "It is no secret what God can do!" The evidences of His healing power are abroad for all to see.

*Sunday*

# What God Can Do

"My God is a living God—sorry about yours!" read the message on the bulletin board in front of a church in a large Southern city. Thank the Lord for such faith in this desolate "God is dead" age! With Job I can also say, "I know that my redeemer liveth." Job 19:25. Two thousand years ago evil men tried to kill God, but their plan failed. They placed Him upon a cross—a dying Saviour—but

He came forth from Joseph's new tomb, triumphant over death.

God is not only living, He is also omnipotent. "All power is given unto me in heaven and in earth," Jesus once declared. (Matthew 28:18.)

"Both riches and honour come of thee," King David prayed, "and thou reignest over all; and in thine hand is power and might; and in thine hand it is to make great, and to give strength unto all." 1 Chronicles 29:12. Such a powerful God is able to care for my few earthly holdings, and my reputation is safe in His overshadowing care. I need not worry.

When the disciples watched their Master calm the angry sea, they looked at each other in amazement, "saying one to another, What manner of man is this! for he commandeth even the winds and water, and they obey him." (Luke 8:25.) The storms of life may rage about me, but peace of heart will be mine when the Master of wind and wave is the pilot of my life's ship.

"God hath power to help," the Good Book affirms. (2 Chronicles 25:8.) After all, this is what most of us need—*help*. We need help in our everyday living, in our relationships with those about us. We need help in solving the problems, in bearing the burdens, in dealing with the cares of our daily lives. We need help in striving to live for Him who died for us. Thank God there *is* help—"God [our living God] hath power to help." This promise is for *you*. It is for *me*.

According to the assurance of His unfailing Word, "God whom we serve is able to deliver." Daniel 3:17. He has power to fulfill His promises. (Romans 4:21.) He has power to make grace abound (2 Corinthians 9:8), "to do exceeding abundantly above all that we ask or think, according to the power that worketh in us" (Ephesians 3:20). He is able "even to subdue all things" (Philippians 3:21), "to keep that which I have committed unto him" (2 Timothy 1:12). He is able to save "to the uttermost" (Hebrews 7:25), and best of all, He is able to keep *me* from falling, and to present *me* "faultless before the presence of his glory with exceeding joy" (Jude 24).

When the dark clouds of some apparently hopeless situation threaten to overwhelm me and to hide God's face, I am reminded of this precious assurance: "With men this is impossible; but with God all things are possible." Matthew 19:26.

You and I need not fear whatever our need may be. We have a living, all-powerful God who loves us and who overshadows us by His mighty power. A God who can create the earth and the beings living on it, who controls the movements of the heavenly bodies throughout the universe, can solve any problem man can possibly encounter.

*Monday*

# Evidences of God's Love

In India I met Jadhav, a hardened criminal who, by his own admission, terrorized his community by deeds of violence. In a fit of anger he had stabbed a man to death. When I met him some time after his arrest, he did not look like a thief or a murderer. He was a quiet, unassuming man with a wholesome, good look about him. Christ had come into Jadhav's life, and a miracle of grace had been performed— grace that changed even a murderer.

In the penal colony of French Guiana where I held gospel meetings some years ago, I met many *libres*—former convicts who had served their prison terms but who were forced to remain in the colony for a period of time before returning to their homeland. Night after night some of those poor specimens of humanity attended the meetings. I saw a complete transformation in the lives of those who accepted Christ, demonstrating that the vilest sinner, who may be guilty of murder, arson, theft, larceny, or treason, can be changed by the grace of God.

In Nyasaland, Africa, I became acquainted with many lepers who, in their physical extremity, have turned to God for help and healing. How my heart went out to those pitiful derelicts of humanity, some with toes and fingers missing, their cheeks puffy, their eyes bloodshot. But the Saviour loves them as much as He loves anyone. If they had been the only members of the human family needing salvation, Jesus would still have cared enough to bear the cross that they might live eternally.

In South Africa I met a woman rescued from what appeared to be hopeless drug addiction. From this living hell God had lifted her and made her a respected, useful member of the community. In this transformed life I saw what the power and grace of God can do to save those who have fallen into the most slavish habits.

But what may be more pertinent is that I have met many persons through the years in different lands who have been saved from evil tempers, from unruly and unkind tongues, from lying, cheating, hatred, bitterness, adultery, profanity, and other evil clutches of the world.

What a blessed assurance these words from the New Testament provide: "Wherefore he is able also to save them to the uttermost that come unto God by him, seeing he ever liveth to make intercession for them." Hebrews 7:25. Thus, you can accept as fact that whatever your need may be today, there is hope for you in Christ. If we accept His aid, nothing is impossible.

# SECTION II

# Something New

I could hardly believe my eyes when I saw what was attributed to Jessamyn West in *The Reader's Digest:*

"If I were to join a circle of any kind, it would be a circle that required its members to *try something new* at least once a month. The new thing could be very inconsequential: steak for breakfast, frog hunting, walking on stilts, memorizing a stanza of poetry. It could be staying up outdoors all night, . . . *reading the Bible—anything not ordinarily done.*"

There it was—"reading the Bible" along with steak for breakfast, frog hunting, walking on stilts, and staying up outdoors all night!

It reminded me of the Malagasy Bible in the British and Foreign Bible Society's interesting collection housed at the Bible House in Queen Victoria Station, London. During a period of great persecution the Queen of Madagascar ordered all Bibles and Christian literature confiscated and burned. The Christians of one village longed to protect the single copy of the Scriptures they had among them. They agreed that the safest place to hide the precious Book was in an artificial cave which served as their smallpox hospital. When the Queen's officers searched the village, they stayed clear of the smallpox hospital, and the villagers' Bible was safe.

Many professed Christians today have tucked their Bibles safely away in some trunk or dark closet to preserve them no doubt from the wear and tear of daily use. Little wonder, then, that Bible reading is considered to be "something new . . . inconsequential . . . [something] not ordinarily done."

One pollster declares that less than one out of ten Americans bother to read the Bible daily. We are turning our backs on the old landmarks which have in the past guided the American people in the way of moral rectitude and spiritual integrity.

Americans, unfortunately, seem to be forgetting the source of power which made theirs a great nation. This beloved country of which we are justly proud was born in the cabin of the ship *Mayflower,* where a handful of brave men undertook to establish a new state founded upon the principles set forth in the Holy Scriptures. Those early Pilgrims made the Word of God the very cornerstone of their homes, the creed of their churches, and the heart of their schools. Their concepts of personal liberty, justice, statecraft, and government found root in a living faith in the divine message. The Declaration of Independence, the Constitution, and the Bill of Rights reflect the teachings of Jesus Christ, whom the early builders of our nation knew and revered.

In the Apostle Paul's day the Bereans were described as "more noble than those in Thessalonica, in that they received the word with all readiness of mind, and searched the scriptures daily." (Acts 17:11.)

Nobility of character—how much each one of us needs the elevating, ennobling influence of God's Word in these days of moral degeneracy, social furor, and spiritual bankruptcy. What a shame to consider reading God's Word "something new . . . inconsequential . . . [something] not ordinarily done"!

With God's help you and I can help change this situation by encouraging our friends to turn back to God's Word. This is the only hope left for the salvation of our nation.

*Wednesday*

# Why the Need of a Bible?

Demosthenes once said, "What we have in us of the image of God is the love of truth and justice." Man through the centuries has pursued a tireless quest for truth. You and I are interested in discovering divine truth, but where can we find it? If we are to discover truth, we must discover the One who is the source of truth. He alone speaks with ultimate authority, and the Book which contains His thoughts is, indeed, the Book of truth.

I believe that the Holy Bible is that Book (John 17:17), for it bears the credentials of divine authority. I believe this Book will lead all who desire to be led to the God of truth. God challenges each of us, "Come now, and let us reason together." Isaiah 1:18.

Why does man need a book through which God may speak to him? Isaiah, the prophet, has the answer: "Your iniquities have separated between you and your God, and your sins have hid his face from you, that he will not hear." Isaiah 59:2.

In the beginning God spoke to a perfect man face to face. Sin separated man from God, his Creator, and the face-to-face communication was broken. Certainly a God who loved man would try to reestablish direct contact with man through some other method. After face-to-face contact became impossible, a God of love surely would not permit the creature of His affection to be forever destroyed without an effort to win him back to faith and loyalty. Is it not reasonable to believe that a divinely inspired book would be one of the media God would use? What *man* would write *about* God could be highly speculative. What *God* would write *to* man would be authoritative.

*Thursday*

# Why Only One Divine Book?

Why does God have only one Book of divine revelation? Would it not be reasonable to expect that He would provide separate guidebooks for people living in Africa, in Asia, in Australia, in Europe, in the Americas, in the islands of the seas? Would not such a wide diversity of nationalities, tribes, and ethnic groups require a variety of holy books to meet the needs of all?

On first thought, such a suggestion sounds plausible, but let us test it further. Luke, the beloved physician of the New Testament, wrote under inspiration that God "hath made of one blood all nations of men for to dwell on all the face of the earth" (Acts 17:26), indicating that mankind is pretty much the same everywhere.

For more than three decades I have associated with peoples from many cultures and levels of education, including those from the most sophisticated areas of earth and those from among the primitive pygmies of the Ituri forest in the Northern Congo. Among all peoples are the good and the bad, the educated and the uneducated, the bright and the dull, the rich and the poor, the saints and the sinners.

Physiologically, peoples of various lands are

much the same—they all require food, water, sunlight, rest, and labor to keep themselves physically fit.

Morally and spiritually, people the world around experience the same need—"There is none righteous, no, not one." "*All* have sinned, and come short of the glory of God." Romans 3:10, 23. *All* need deliverance from the guilt and bondage of sin. *All* need restoration to that state that was man's when he came forth from the hand of the Creator. One plan—the plan of redemption—will meet the needs of men of all ages and from all nations. Only one Book—the God-inspired Book, the Bible—can reveal that blessed plan with its all-sufficient Saviour, and it is readily available to every one of us today.

*Friday*

# Myth or Masterpiece?

During World War II and the subsequent fighting in Korea and Vietnam, the Bible has become a new Book to thousands of boys risking their lives on the battlefield. Men who face death realize that nothing prepares them for that supreme ordeal as do the promises of God recorded in the Book of books. In the foxholes, in bomber and fighter planes, above or below the tossing waves of the seas, wherever men do battle, the Bible has faithfully borne its silent but mighty witness. It has a living message for these times because it is the Word of the living God. (1 Thessalonians 2:13.)

Only God could have directed the production of a book such as the Bible. Here we have sixty-six volumes written by some forty different authors. These men of God spoke many different languages and came from varied estates of life. There was Moses, the adopted son of an Egyptian princess. There was David, the shepherd boy, who later became one of the greatest kings of Israel. There were a prime minister, a tax collector, a herdsman, a physician, several fishermen. These men lived and wrote over a period of fifteen hundred years.

Think, too, of the wide range of areas in which they wrote—music, history, science, and religion.

From such a heterogeneous array we would expect to find sharply conflicting opinions. Such would definitely be the results of mere human authorship, but a careful study of the Bible reveals no such contradictions. A perfect thread of harmony runs through the sixty-six books, each writer unconsciously confirming the words of his predecessor, his contemporary, or his successor. This consistent harmony can mean but one thing—the same omnipresent Spirit directed the work of each writer.

Moses did not write his own words, nor did David, Isaiah, John, or Paul. They wrote what was revealed to them by the Holy Spirit of God, who changes not. Thus contradiction and confusion are eliminated, and the harmony of the Bible is one of the outstanding proofs of its divine inspiration.

*Saturday*

# The Source of Light and Understanding

Someone once asked Sun Yat-sen, a political leader in China in 1912, when the great awakening of China began.

"It began when Robert Morrison translated the Bible into Chinese," was his reply.

Thinking men from all walks of life and of all ages have recognized the worth and the power of the Bible. Sir Isaac Newton, British scientist and philosopher, described the gospel as "the most sublime philosophy" on earth. Patrick Henry, fiery American patriot, declared that God's Word was "a Book worth all other books." Other eminent American leaders such as Benjamin Franklin, Abraham Lincoln, Franklin D. Roosevelt, and Dwight D. Eisenhower have paid high tribute to the power of the Holy Scriptures.

Dr. J. Wilbur Chapman wrote this glowing tribute to the Bible: "There's none like it when your head is aching! There is none like it when your heart is breaking! There is none like it when the day is without the sun and the night without its star! There is none like it when your children are motherless! There is none like it when you bury your baby! There's none like it when you reach the end of life's journey and pillow your head on its promises and God stoops and kisses you to sleep."

We live in a spiritually dark and morally confused world. How much we need the guiding, healing light of God's Word!

"Thy word is a lamp unto my feet, and a light unto my path," the psalmist declared in Psalm 119: 105. "The entrance of thy words giveth light; it giveth understanding unto the simple." Verse 130.

May we follow the rays of this blessed lamp faithfully, for then and only then will we have true light and understanding.

*Sunday*

# A Book of the Future

"Sahib, I can see that you are a very lucky man. Let me tell your fortune!" The bearded Oriental mystic, clutching a small satchel containing his

stock-in-trade, sidled up to my car parked near busy
Crawford Market in Bombay, India.

"I can see that you are going on a long journey,"
he continued persistently, "and you will become
very rich."

I had heard this line many times before from the
glib Eastern soothsayers. I have indeed taken many
long journeys, not a few before I met my fortune-
telling friend in Bombay. But pantalooned prophets
of the East have missed the mark when they foretold
great wealth for me.

"Boast not thyself of to morrow," the wise man
of the Bible reminds us; "for thou knowest not what
a day may bring forth." Proverbs 27:1. Man alone
cannot tell what lies beyond tomorrow. When we
find a book that accurately foretells the future and
history records exact fulfillment, we may know that
book was not written by man alone. God had a part
in directing the authors.

Evidence of the divine origin of the Holy Scriptures is both ample and convincing. "Remember the
former things of old: for I am God, and there is
none else; I am God, and there is none like me, declaring the end from the beginning, and from ancient times the things that are not yet done, saying,
My counsel shall stand, and I will do all my pleasure." Isaiah 46:9, 10. With God the future is present and He alone is able to declare accurately what

the next day, the next year, or the next century will reveal.

Years, sometimes centuries, before the events took place, Bible writers foretold experiences that would befall individuals, cities, nations, and religious powers. Some of these we shall deal with later in this volume. Inspired by the gift of prophecy, authors of the Word have described even the very days in which we live and have explained their meaning. Divine prophecy draws aside the curtain that separates time from eternity, and depicts the eternal home of the redeemed. We may have confidence in the prophecies of the Bible because of the unerring accuracy with which some portions of the prophetic Word have already come to pass. "For the prophecy came not in old time by the will of man: but holy men of God spake as they were moved by the Holy Ghost." 2 Peter 1:21. Biblical prophecy comes not from men's educated guesses but from God's ability to foretell the future. He created the universe and knows its destiny.

This blessed Book—the Bible—must indeed be God's Book, for it has foretold with amazing accuracy events long before they came to pass. Only God can see the future; only God's Book can speak with certainty of things yet to come. Fulfilled and fulfilling prophecy is a mighty evidence of the divine authorship of the Holy Scriptures.

*Monday*

# The Reliability of Prophecy

We were visiting Nebbi Yunus in Iraq. We looked out through a small latticed window which framed the mounds of Kuyunjik in the distance. There before us was Bible prophecy fulfilled. There was framed a fact no unbeliever could gainsay. The mounds of ancient Nineveh stand today as mute but convincing testimony of the trustworthiness of Bible prophecy.

Many centuries earlier while Nineveh was enjoying her heyday of power, the prophet Zephaniah once foretold the city's doom: "He will stretch out his hand against the north, and destroy Assyria; and *will make Nineveh a desolation, and dry like a wilderness.*" Zephaniah 2:13.

We saw what had been the proud city of Nineveh now indeed a "desolation, and dry like a wilderness." "With an overrunning flood he will make an utter end of the place," the prophet Nahum foretold of Nineveh at the height of its power. (Nahum 1: 8.) Perhaps given a glimpse of the desolation that is Nineveh today, the prophet cried, "She is empty, and void, and waste." Nahum 2:10.

How did Zephaniah and Nahum know that the mighty city of Nineveh would be totally destroyed?

The destruction of Nineveh in the days of the prophets seemed as farfetched as it would be for someone
in our day to foretell the fall of our great metropolis
on the Eastern Seaboard. But Nineveh fell!

How did Zephaniah and Nahum know of the
fall of the city years before it took place? God revealed it to them. He alone can look into the future
and declare events before they come to pass: "Remember the former things of old: for I am God, and
there is none else; I am God, and there is none like
me, declaring the end from the beginning, and from
ancient times the things that are not yet done, saying, My counsel shall stand, and I will do all my
pleasure." Isaiah 46:9, 10.

For years I had heard and read about Tyre, the
once-proud city at the eastern end of the Mediter-
ranean in what today is the country of Lebanon.
I had never expected to visit this part of the world,
but here I was—but where was Tyre? I was not surprised to find barren rocks and fishing nets spread
out to dry. I had read the prophetic portions of the
Bible regarding the fate of this wicked metropolis.
It was just as I expected, just as the Scriptures
foretold.

Centuries before Christ lived, when Tyre was a
bustling commercial center, the prophet Ezekiel in-
scribed on a scroll that the godless city would be
destroyed, that the very dust of her ruins would be

scraped so that she would become like the top of a rock, a place for the spreading of nets. "And I will make thee like the top of a rock: thou shalt be a place to spread nets upon; thou shalt be built no more: for I the Lord have spoken it, saith the Lord God." Ezekiel 26:14.

Tyre was first destroyed by Nebuchadnezzar and his Babylonian army. It remained for Alexander the Great, however, to complete the total destruction of the city, leaving it like the top of a rock. His soldiers took the walls, the towers, and the timber from the ruined houses and palaces of ancient Tyre and built a causeway for an attack on the new island city that had appeared after the attack of the Babylonians. So great was the demand for material that the very dust of the old ruins was scraped and laid in the sea. To this day the site of the ancient city on the mainland is as bare as the top of a rock whereon fishermen spread their nets. What a truly marvelous fulfillment of Bible prophecy!

*Tuesday*

# Words to Meet Man's Need

"What a wonderful Book this is!" exclaimed a learned Chinese employed to translate the Bible into one of the dialects of his country.

"Why do you say that?" asked a surprised friend.

"Because," replied the scholar, "it tells me so very much about myself. It seems to know all about me. The One who made this Book must be the One who made me."

The Bible *is* a wonderful Book. It is a true Book. It is a fact-filled, interest-packed Book. Its contents range through theology, history, science, philosophy, ethnology, ethics, romance, drama, public and personal relations, and other topics that have captured human interest and attention through the centuries.

The Bible is more than a good or true book, however. Man may write a good book, a true book, even a wonderful book, but man has never produced a volume that compares with the Holy Scriptures. The Bible *lives!* Through its sacred pages God moves and speaks to human hearts. It is a Book of divine origin destined from the beginning to fill a unique need among the human family. No other volume has successfully challenged it.

In fact, the Apostle Paul declares, "All scripture is given by inspiration of God, and is profitable for doctrine, for reproof, for correction, for instruction in righteousness: that the man of God may be perfect, throughly furnished unto all good works." 2 Timothy 3:16, 17.

God gave mankind the Bible to guide them in this life and prepare them for the one to come.

John Wesley said, "I want to know one thing—
the way to heaven, how to land on that happy shore.
God Himself has condescended to teach the way;
for this very end He came from heaven. He hath
written it down in a book! O give me that book! At
any price, give me that book of God! I have it; here
is knowledge enough for me. Let me be a man of
one Book."

We, too, should cry out with John Wesley, "O
give us that Book! At any price, give us that Book
of God!"

*Wednesday*

# Don't Be Content With a Brass Egg

An ancient prince sent a gift to his betrothed.
When the young lady received the gift from the
hands of the royal messenger, she was incensed, for
it was an iron egg. Indignantly throwing the crude
object to the ground, she was about to rush angrily
to her room when she noticed the iron egg had
been opened slightly by the fall. Picking it up, she
discovered a brass egg inside. Examining it curi-
ously, she touched a spring that caused the brass
egg to open, revealing a silver egg. The key to these
delightful discoveries in hand, she found a gold egg
encasing a magnificent diamond.

Did you ever try to read the Bible only to find it a bit dry and uninteresting? Perhaps the unfamiliar phraseology sometimes dismayed you, and you had a hard time following the train of thought. Did the figures of speech puzzle you? Did the stories seem strange and amazing, maybe even unlike anything you had read before? After a brief attempt, you probably threw it aside, convinced that there was nothing in it for you.

You may be like a friend of mine in South Africa. During the rush for diamonds some decades ago, John Cooks staked out a claim and began to dig. His area yielded a few small stones, but after days of toil and sweat, he gave it up as a poor investment. Years later he said to me, "You know, another chap came in later, went a few feet deeper, and found his fortune. I stopped digging too soon."

It may be that you have stopped digging too soon, for gold and precious gems are in that mine of truth, the Bible. It could be that you are tampering with the iron egg and have yet to discover the greater treasure of diamonds inside. Don't stop too soon. Your fortune may be just a little deeper. "If thou seekest her as silver, and searchest for her as for hid treasures; then shalt thou understand the fear of the Lord, and find the knowledge of God." Proverbs 2:4, 5. Don't be content with a brass egg, and don't stop digging too soon.

*Thursday*

# He Couldn't Use It Because He Didn't Know

In a church paper I once read an interesting story sent to the editor by a reader. I would like to share this with you. It just might prove helpful.

"On a hilly farm near New Gloucester [Maine] . . . there once lived a young man named Orin Beggs, who was fed up with trying to make things grow in soil that was mostly rocks.

" 'I'm going to New York City,' he told his parents one day.

" 'You're making a mistake,' said his father. 'Don't ever write for money unless it's for carfare home.'

"Next day, as the young man was about to get on the train, his mother handed him a Bible with a leather cover and a brass clasp.

" 'If you ever get discouraged,' she said, 'read the 115th Psalm. It's sure to bring you comfort. . . .'

"The depression of the late 90's was getting under way, and Orin found that getting a job in New York wasn't as easy as he had figured. The question was always the same: 'What can you do?'—and all the farm boy was good at was milking cows and hoeing potatoes.

"The few dollars Orin had saved went pretty fast, and a month after his arrival in the big town he spent his last dime for a roll and a glass of milk. . . .

"Finally too weak to walk any more, he gave up and wired his father collect for train fare home.

"His parents were at the New Gloucester station to meet him, and after he had had his first square meal in weeks his mother took him upstairs to help him unpack his suitcase.

" 'I'm sorry it turned out this way,' she said.

" 'I had a job waiting for me,' said Orin, 'if I could have held out another week. But I just got too tired and hungry.'

" 'Did you open the Bible I gave you?' his mother asked.

" 'No,' said her son. 'When I got discouraged, it was money I needed, not Bible reading.'

"His mother undid the brass clasp and opened the Good Book to the 115th Psalm. There, pressed between the India-paper pages, was a $50 bill."

Perhaps there is something you and I need more than we need a $50 bill, and we just might find it in the same Book that held the money Orin Beggs couldn't use because he didn't know it was there, for he never got around to opening the Bible.

It is worth looking into, at least. (Jeremiah 15:16.)

*Friday*

# Yoga, Guru, or What Have You

Yoga, Guru, Swami, Vedanta—American papers occasionally contain these mystic terms well known to those of us who have spent years in the Orient. Ancient Oriental rites are now being translated into "pop-culture fads" here in the United States. But I have gotten ahead of my story. Before we pursue the gurus, let us recall the few minutes we spent with a friend yesterday—Orin Beggs, who couldn't enjoy fifty dollars for a very good reason—he didn't know it was in the Bible his mother gave him.

The story reminds me of these words written by an ancient prophet who lived many centuries ago: "My people are destroyed for lack of knowledge: because thou hast rejected knowledge, I will also reject thee, that thou shalt be no priest to me: seeing thou hast forgotten the law of thy God, I will also forget thy children." Hosea 4:6.

The marginal reading of this verse says, "My people are 'cut off' for lack of knowledge." Do you see the connection? Orin Beggs was in desperate financial straits. He needed money badly. The money was available, but he couldn't use it because he didn't know it was in his possession.

How many people are searching for peace, for contentment! How many need encouragement, wisdom, understanding! In their restless quest for help, for fulfillment, countless youth today turn to the exotic subcultures of big-city life. They learn the "cobra pose," the "sun exercise," or the "corpse pose." They sit cross-legged on hard floors in dim rooms bedecked with peacock feathers. They sway and chant. They repeat unvarying lyrics by the hour. Why? In search of "bliss"—in search of something they do not have. Unfortunately, too few of their parents or adult acquaintances have what they are searching for, either.

Peace and happiness may be yours for the asking, for the searching. The answer to human need is not to be found in the yoga den or the mystic's pad; not in the *Bhagavad-Gita* or some other Sanskrit holy book. It will be found in God's living Book, the Bible. Hundreds of thousands search for the little-known writings of mystical cults and religions and avidly read them. But few study the Bible. Within its sacred pages the honest searcher for truth will find help for every need, but he must know where to find it and how to appropriate that help if he is to make use of it. When one neglects to study the Word, he cuts himself off from the source of blessing and help in time of need. In fact, he is very much like Orin Beggs and his fifty dollars.

*Saturday*

# Famine Ahead!

"U.S. Scientist Warns of World Famine," a head-line in our newspaper stated on September 2, 1964. "It will be the most colossal catastrophe in history," Dr. R. Ewell, vice-president for research, New York State University, in Buffalo, was quoted as predict-ing, "and hundreds of millions and even billions of human beings will be stricken.

"Such a famine in Asia, Africa, and South America by the 1970's and later seems almost in-evitable," Dr. Ewell declared, and he then explained that the population explosion in the world today will in time outstrip food production.

I have visited famine-stricken areas in the Ori-ent. It is a haunting experience—men, women, and little children slowly dying for lack of food.

God's Word, however, speaks of a terrible famine ahead: "Behold, the days come, saith the Lord God, that I will send a famine in the land, not a famine of bread, nor a thirst for water, but of hearing the words of the Lord: and they shall wan-der from sea to sea, and from the north even to the east, they shall run to and fro to seek the word of the Lord, and shall not find it." Amos 8:11, 12.

Here the prophet paints a picture of famine, not

of bread, "but of hearing the words of the Lord." He depicts a time when men and women will wander "from sea to sea, and from the north even to the east" searching for "the word of the Lord, and shall not find it."

"Then shall they call upon me, but I will not answer; they shall seek me early, but they shall not find me: for that they hated knowledge, and did not choose the fear of the Lord: they would none of my counsel: they despised all my reproof. Therefore shall they eat of the fruit of their own way, and be filled with their own devices." Proverbs 1:28-31.

It is terrible to see men and women without physical food to sustain their bodies. It is equally terrible when human beings who have had the opportunity of studying God's Word but have failed to take advantage of it find themselves starving for the Bread of Life.

Little wonder that the Old Testament prophet Isaiah entreats, "Seek ye the Lord while he may be found, call ye upon him while he is near." Isaiah 55:6.

Now, while we have God's Word to study freely, we need to apply ourselves diligently to its study, lest a time of famine find us unprepared.

# SECTION III

# "What Think Ye?"

"What think YE of Christ?" This is the greatest question facing every human being.

There are many important issues before the world's leaders at this time. Daily the United Nations wrestles with matters of great moment. What will be the outcome of the trouble in the Far East? How will the nagging crisis in the Middle East be resolved? Will the emerging nations of Africa be successful in establishing stable, representative governments? Which side will win the battle of the Titans—the East or the West?

These are vital questions. It is important that right answers be found to each of them. But the greatest question before us as individuals today is, "What think ye of Christ?" Matthew 22:42. Our response to this question will determine our ultimate destiny—where we will spend eternity.

An atheist lay dying. For him death was but a leap into the night, the falling of a dark curtain of finality. It was the end. Without Jesus, there was no coming Life-giver, no glorious resurrection morning. As he pondered some of these realities on his deathbed, evidently the Spirit of God was at work upon his heart, for found among his papers after his

death were these words which have since been put
to music:

> "I've tried in vain a thousand ways
> My fears to quell, my hopes to raise;
> But what I need, the Bible says,
> Is ever, only Jesus.

> "My soul is night, my heart is steel,
> I cannot see, I cannot feel;
> For light, for life, I must appeal
> In simple faith to Jesus.

> "He died, He lives, He reigns, He pleads;
> There's love in all His words and deeds;
> There's all a guilty sinner needs
> Forevermore in Jesus.

> "Though some should sneer, and some
>     should blame,
> I'll go with all my guilt and shame;
> I'll go to Him because His name
> Above all names, is Jesus."

James Converse, A

The knights, checking the shield, found that each
side contained a different heraldic design.

*Monday*

# Both God and Man

Centuries ago two knights met in front of a castle. The owner of the estate was a wealthy nobleman whose ancestral shield was affixed to a high post on the roadside.

"Did you notice His Lordship's coat of arms as you passed?" one knight asked.

"Yes," replied the other.

"What was on it?" the first knight said.

The second horseman described what he had seen.

"But you are wrong, sir!" replied the other. "I read it distinctly," and he proceeded to tell what he had read.

An argument followed, tempers flared, and the two were about to come to blows when a stranger rode up. Learning what the quarrel was about, he suggested they both go and read together.

The knights followed his advice. They discovered both were right. The shield had two sides. The knights had approached from opposite directions. The inscriptions on the two sides were different. Actually each had only half the truth. There were two sides to the question.

We need to know the whole truth about the

Lord Jesus Christ. The Bible reveals two sides to His life. He was man. He was God. As man, the Bible pictures Him possessing many of the frailties of human flesh. He became weary. He became hungry. He sought human love and sympathy.

The Inspired Word also pictures Him as God, forgiving sins, healing diseases, commanding the forces of nature, even raising the dead. Both pictures are equally true. Jesus was more than a good man; He was the God-man!

*How* Jesus could be both God and man I cannot explain. Paul calls it "the mystery of godliness": "And without controversy great is the mystery of godliness: God was manifest in the flesh, justified in the Spirit, seen of angels, preached unto the Gentiles, believed on in the world, received up into glory." 1 Timothy 3:16.

If we could explain all the mysteries of the nature of God, we would be equal with Him. Some things we will not understand until we meet Him in the earth made new.

Our finite minds cannot fathom all the questions of the Godhead or understand how Jesus could at once be both God and man. But we do know well *why* He took man's nature: "For God so loved the world, that he gave his only begotten Son, that whosoever believeth in him should not perish, but have everlasting life." John 3:16.

Love found a way to deal with mankind's greatest affliction—*sin*.

*Tuesday*

# Christ Prior to Eden

Before the Wise Men brought their gifts to the
Babe in Bethlehem's manger, before the ark of
Noah plowed its way through the angry waters of
the Flood, before Adam and Eve were driven from
the Garden of God, before the world came forth
from the hand of the Creator, the Son of God was in
existence. This is indicated in a prayer Jesus prayed:

"O Father, glorify thou me with thine own self
with the glory which I had with thee before the
world was." John 17:5. Here the Saviour speaks of
a fellowship with the Father before the foundations
of the world were laid.

In fact, the inspired writers of the New Testament make it clear that Jesus, the Son of God, was,
indeed, the Creator of the world. "For by him were
all things created, that are in heaven, and that are in
earth, visible and invisible, whether they be thrones,
or dominions, or principalities, or powers: all things
were created by him, and for him: and he is before
all things, and by him all things consist." Colossians
1:16, 17.

Paul again writes of Christ the Son, "The heavens are the works of thine hands." Hebrews 1:10. At night when you look into the starry heavens, those glowing galaxies of God, remember that these are the works of His hands.

Isaac Watts wrote:

"He formed the stars, those heavenly flames,
He counts their numbers, calls their names;
His wisdom's vast, and knows no bound,
A deep where all our thoughts are drowned."

Jesus Christ is far more than the son of Mary with influence. He is indeed the Son of God with power!

*Wednesday*

# Christ's Biography Written Before His Birth!

Jesus Christ is the only one ever to fulfill the Messianic prophecies of the Old Testament. Take your Bible and look up the prophecies, then look up the record of their fulfillment indicated by the texts which follow:

| | |
|---|---|
| Hosea 11:1 | The flight into Egypt foretold. |
| Matthew 2:14 | Fulfilled in the life of Jesus Christ. |

| | |
|---|---|
| Isaiah 53:3 | His reception at the hands of His own people. |
| John 1:11 | Came to His own—His own received Him not. |
| Psalm 41:9 | To be betrayed by a friend. |
| Mark 14:10 | Judas Iscariot, one of His own, betrays Christ. |
| Zechariah 11:12 | Christ's price to be thirty pieces of silver. |
| Matthew 26:15 | Covenanted with priests for thirty pieces of silver. |
| Isaiah 53:12 | "Numbered with the transgressors." |
| Matthew 27:38 | Christ crucified between two thieves. |
| Psalm 22:18 | Would cast lots for His clothing. |
| Mark 15:24 | Soldiers part His garments. |
| Isaiah 53:9 | Would be buried with the rich. |
| Matthew 27:57-60 | Jesus in Joseph's new tomb. |
| Psalm 16:10 | The grave would not be able to hold Him. |
| Matthew 28:5-10 | Jesus after His resurrection. |
| Psalm 68:18 | His ascension foretold. |
| Luke 24:50, 51 | Christ ascends. |

There can be no mistake; Jesus Christ was indeed the long-awaited Messiah of the Scriptures. More than this, He is *your* Saviour and *mine* down here in the twentieth century. He can and will meet our every need.

*Thursday*

# From Convicted Murderer to Converted Saint

Early Sunday morning on idyllic St. Croix, one of the Virgin Islands, the Caribbean sun was just peeping through gently waving palms as several hundred of us gathered on the edge of a lagoon to witness a baptismal service.

Up rumbled a drab pickup with markings of the nearby United States prison on the cab. A warden stepped out, and with him a huge hulk of a man dressed in prison garb. Rochester, I learned, was a "lifer." Some years earlier he had brutally murdered his employer. Today he was to be baptized.

As the pastor and the prisoner waded slowly into the water, I turned to the warden.

"Tell me, Officer," I said, "has that man truly been converted, or is this just a way of having things easier inside?"

"Preacher," the warden replied, "if I have ever

seen a converted man, Rochester is that man. When he came to the prison, he was the most incorrigible individual I had ever met. He was surly, uncooperative, and took delight in making things rough for us. Then the young people from your church came to conduct religious services at the prison. At first Rochester would not attend the meetings, but gradually a change came over him. He not only listened, but took part in the services. Today he is a model prisoner—cooperative, cheerful, helpful, anxious to please. Yes, Preacher, Rochester is a changed man."

Thank God for the gospel of the Lord Jesus Christ that changes the hearts and lives of men— even of confessed murderers! It changes the old life: "Therefore if any man be in Christ, he is a new creature: old things are passed away; behold, all things are become new." 2 Corinthians 5:17.

*Friday*

# The Devil Pays Well

A man and a woman were standing at the bus stop, the woman carrying an oversize shopping bag.

"May I help you, ma'am?" the man asked kindly as he offered to hold the bag.

"Well—er—thank you," the woman stammered

as the man took the bag. But he did not tarry long. Looking quickly around, he dashed behind the nearest building with the heavy parcel.

The woman stood aghast for a moment, then broke out in a loud laugh.

"That's a good one on him," she said to another woman who had seen the robbery. "I had a dead dog in that bag. I was on my way to the country to bury it. What a surprise he has in store!"

That thief's pay for his crime was a dead dog.

The Apostle Paul speaks of other pay—other wages: "The wages of sin is *death*." Romans 6:23. "Sin *pays* its servants," J. B. Phillips translates Paul's words; "the wage is death."

The devil pays his workmen exactly what they earn. "The soul that sinneth, it shall die." Ezekiel 18:4. The death that Paul and Ezekiel write of is not the natural death all die. This death is the result of sin. The wages of sin are an eternal death, a death from which there is no resurrection. Inspired writers call it the "second death." (Revelation 20:6.)

In this final destruction when sin and sinners are destroyed, the wicked will receive only that which they themselves have chosen. God made plain before them the way of life and the way of death. We receive exactly what we ourselves have chosen. It is a very sobering thought. But the story does not end here.

*Saturday*

# Christ Died Even for Terrorists

One December morning in 1967 I was speaking to a group of Viet Cong prisoners in a Vietnamese prison camp. The front veranda of a Buddhist temple served as my rostrum. On a banner stretched above my head were the words of Paul to the Philippian jailer, "Believe on the Lord Jesus Christ, and thou shalt be saved." Acts 16:31.

Before me that morning were forty-eight men who some months earlier had been plotters, arsonists, terrorists, thieves, and murderers. Now they were transformed into peaceful, lovable Christians. They were presenting themselves for baptism and membership in the Seventh-day Adventist Church. Television and radio stations and the press heralded their conversion around the world.

What power had wrought this great change in their lives? Who had taken away the burden of their guilt and condemnation? In short, who had assumed the penalty for their sin and transgression?

The only possible answer is simply and certainly Jesus Christ, the Man of Calvary. The Apostle Paul wrote, "We can see that it was while we were powerless to help ourselves that Christ died for sinful men." Romans 5:6, Phillips. Christ died for Viet

Cong as He died for Americans, for sinners from every land. Sinners in every land deserve to die. They are marked men. The penalty of death hangs inexorably over their heads. That penalty must be paid.

Thank God Paul's words do not end there. He also assures the sinner that "the gift of God is eternal life through Jesus Christ our Lord." (Romans 6:23.)

"The gift of God"—this is what the Viet Cong needed. It is what you and I need. If we are not to die, someone else must be our substitute and pay the penalty, for the claims of God's law must be satisfied.

*Sunday*

# Three Choices of God

When Adam sinned, the penalty for his transgression passed upon the human race. "In Adam all die." 1 Corinthians 15:22. On the awful day that Adam sinned, God had three choices. He could ignore Adam's sin. He could blot man out of existence. He could provide a way of escape.

For God to ignore sin would be to impugn His *justice*. To destroy mankind would call in question His *love*. Therefore God found a way of escape for sinful man. The penalty could be paid only by One equal to God. An angel, a created being, could not pay the awful debt. He could not come from the tomb as a conqueror over death. Christ alone, God's only-begotten Son, could assume the debt, could pay the price, and then come forth victor over fallen man's most implacable enemy—death. Both Father and Son were willing. "For God so loved the world, that he gave his only begotten Son." John 3:16. "Christ reconciled us to God by *dying for us*." Romans 5:10, Phillips.

This is only a very crude illustration, but it may help us to understand what is involved in the payment of man's debt by Christ: You owe a businessman one thousand dollars. Misfortune has befallen you, so you cannot pay. You are threatened with dire consequences. A friend takes pity on you—and hands you a valid check for one thousand dollars. Provision for paying the debt is made. You hold in your hand a check which you may cash and obtain money to pay the debt, or which you may ignore and suffer the consequences. The decision is up to you. As no one can cash another's check without the person's permission, so God cannot save us without our consent.

When by faith we decide to accept the payment already made for our sin, we in effect cash the check. Our debt of sin is paid.

*Monday*

# The Meaning of Justification

Justification, in a religious sense, is a big word with a very simple meaning. It is, however, a very important word, for it deals with our past life and our salvation. When our past sins are forgiven, we are "justified."

The Apostle John sums up justification in these words: "If we confess our sins, he is faithful and just to forgive us our sins, and to cleanse us from all unrighteousness." 1 John 1:9.

We surrender, we repent, we confess our sins. We believe Christ forgives those sins. By faith we accept His death upon the cross as our substitute, as payment of the penalty for our sin. Our faith lays hold of this blessed fact, and because we believe, He makes it a glorious reality. Because Jesus died, because He has forgiven our sins, we then stand before God as though we had never sinned. His blood cleanses us "from all unrighteousness."

It is not something that *we* have done that restores us to favor with God. It is what *God, through Christ,* has done for us. We have not earned either the pardon or the cleansing. Both are *gifts* of God. We receive them by faith. These gifts wipe clean the marred record of our past. We stand forgiven, cleansed, and justified before the tribunal of heaven.

"Under this divine 'system' a man who has faith is now freely acquitted in the eyes of God by his generous dealing in the redemptive act of Christ Jesus." Romans 3:24, Phillips.

One Christian writer declares, "The enemy of man and God is not willing that this truth [justification by faith] should be clearly presented; for he knows that if the people receive it fully, his power will be broken."—Quoted by A. G. Daniells in *Christ Our Righteousness*, p. 54.

God can break the power of evil in our lives and assure our salvation if we are willing for Him to do so. Then this big word *justification* will assume new significance, new meaning, for it will be embodied within the context of a close spiritual relationship between us and God.

*Tuesday*

## "The Victory Is Ours"

"The victory is ours, thank God!" the Apostle Paul exults. "He makes it ours by our Lord Jesus Christ." 1 Corinthians 15:57, Moffatt. And Christ Himself gives us this encouraging word: "In the world ye shall have tribulation: but be of good cheer; I have overcome the world." John 16:33.

"Lo, I am with you alway, even unto the end of the world." Matthew 28:20.

Years ago a man needed eye surgery. Restoration of his sight would require a delicate and costly operation. The surgeon's fee would be some five thousand dollars. This amount the poor man was unable to pay.

"Can't you reduce this fee for a man as poor as I am?" he pleaded with the surgeon.

"I am sorry," replied the specialist; "I cannot lower my fees." The poor man's hopes fell, but the doctor continued, "However, I can and I will perform this surgery for you free of charge."

In the spiritual realm Christ does for us what the compassionate surgeon did for the blind man—He gives His services to us without cost so that we may be made whole. We do not merit His help. We cannot earn the life of victory in our own strength, but help comes from above, free of charge.

How is this possible? Christ promises that He will permit no temptation to come our way "but such as is common to man." He "will not suffer you to be tempted above that ye are able; but will with the temptation also make a way to escape, that ye may be able to bear it." (1 Corinthians 10:13.) He strengthens us. (Ephesians 3:16.) He provides grace to enable us to overcome sin. (2 Corinthians 12:9.) The angels of God are at the disposal of the heirs of salvation (Hebrews 1:14), and Jesus Himself prays for us (Luke 22:31, 32). How can we fail?

The victory is ours. Thank God, He makes it ours through the Lord Jesus Christ. Daily victory —this is true sanctification.

*Wednesday*

# Help for Today's Struggle

It is not enough to know that our dark yesterdays are cared for. The imputed righteousness of Christ blotted out our past sins. But what of the present? There is today's battle against temptation that we must win. It is not enough that we merely begin the Christian life. Jesus Himself declared that only "the man who holds out to the end will be saved." (Matthew 24:13, Phillips.)

We need help every day of our lives to maintain a right relationship with our fellowmen and with God. Daily we must be growing more and more like the Master of our lives, and this experience of growth and emulation is called sanctification. Unlike justification, which is a transaction of a moment, sanctification is a work of growth lasting a lifetime.

Is there help here for us in this matter of sanctification? Thank God, there is. The same Christ who died to care for our past sins has supplied, through His perfect life, the strength and help we need to live victorious, overcoming lives on a day-by-day basis.

"The Lord knows how to rescue a good man surrounded by temptation," Peter declares. (2 Peter 2:9, Phillips.) "My grace is sufficient for thee," Jesus told the afflicted Paul. (2 Corinthians 12:9.) Thus for our present needs as well as for our past mistakes we can depend completely upon Christ for the help we need, for He knows how to help us. And He who created this planet and its living creatures has *infinite power* to help us.

If the crucified Christ is sufficient for the past, the indwelling Christ supplies grace in abundance sufficient for the present. "If we love one another God does actually live within us, and his love grows in us toward perfection." 1 John 4:12, Phillips. Here in these words is found the secret of daily victorious living, for by loving our fellowmen we make it possible for God to become a loving reality within us, a source of power strong enough to enable us to stand unmoved in the presence of any temptation.

"He gives us grace potent enough to meet . . . every . . . evil spirit." James 4:6, Phillips. This promise is for you.

*Thursday*

# Not by Proxy

"Though Noah, Daniel, and Job, were in it, as I live, saith the Lord God, they shall deliver neither son nor daughter; they shall but deliver their own souls by their righteousness." Ezekiel 14:20.

God has made ample provision for all men to be saved. Christ has suffered "death for every man." (Hebrews 2:9.)

The Spirit of God issues this invitation to men and women, old and young, from every clime and from every age: "Let him that is athirst come. And whosoever will, let him take of the water of life freely." Revelation 22:17.

But we must individually respond to this invitation. We cannot be saved by the godliness of someone else. A godly father or mother, a Christian brother or sister, son or daughter, no matter how close to the Lord such may live, cannot save us. "Character is not transferable. No man can believe for another. No man can receive the Spirit for another. No man can impart to another the character which is the fruit of the Spirit's working."—Ellen G. White, *Christ's Object Lessons,* p. 412.

Noah, Daniel, and Job were men of God. They lived and served the Lord in difficult places, under

trying circumstances, and they remained steadfast
and true in the face of opposition and persecution.
There was no question about the closeness of their
relationship to God. But, as the prophet says, "they
shall deliver neither son nor daughter." Their stead-
fastness, their consecration, could not save even
their own children. Their sons and daughters had
to make their own decisions. They had to establish
their own connection with God. The godly influence
of their parents no doubt greatly helped and inspired
them, but their own experiences with God had to be
nonetheless real, nonetheless personal.

There is no salvation by proxy. Every man must
stand or fall by his own experience in the day of
judgment.

# SECTION IV

Jim Padgett, Art

Christ accepts us back—though we do not deserve
it—as the father welcomed the prodigal son.

*Friday*

# The Voice of Conscience

According to little Henry in kindergarten, the conscience is "what tells us when *Billy* does wrong." But the Scriptures tell us conscience is a voice within each individual to guide each person into the way of life eternal.

In the midst of our godless or careless way, a voice deep inside speaks to our hearts. This voice of love "reproves" or "convinces" us of sin. (John 16: 8.) A gnawing, persistent conscience reminds us that we are on the wrong road, that "the wages of sin is death." (Romans 6:23.) If we persist in our wrong ways, we are "without Christ, being aliens from the commonwealth of Israel, and strangers from the covenants of promise, having no hope, and without God in the world." (Ephesians 2:12.) Summed up in three words of doom—*we are lost*.

Thank God, Heaven does not leave us on a dead-end street. The same Spirit which reveals our lost condition also points us to a loving Saviour. He is lifted up before us in all of His beauty and loveliness. We see Him upon the cross dying for us personally.

A glimpse of ourselves, our poor, sinful selves; a long look at our Saviour, who, thank God, can

86

and will save us "to the uttermost"—and we are on our way to peace of mind, purity of heart, and ultimately to glorification of body. (1 John 3:2.)

A sensitive conscience will indeed tell little Billy when he has done something wrong, but such a conscience will also tell little Henry the same thing—about himself.

*Saturday*

# What Repentance Is All About

"Except ye repent, ye shall all . . . perish." It is just that awesomely simple. Jesus Himself said so. (Luke 13:3.) There is no easy, more pleasant way. There are no detours—no circuitous routes to the kingdom. It is either repent or perish.

Repentance may be a humiliating experience. In fact, true repentance is bound to be. It lays our vaunted ego in the dust, and self suffers a humiliating, crushing defeat. But the Saviour says that we must either repent or perish!

The Latin term from which our English word *repent* comes means "to creep back." And that is just what true repentance means—"to creep back." After we have seen our real selves in the light of Calvary's drama, we are on our knees in contrition —and on our knees all we can do is creep.

The Old Testament prophet Ezra knew what true repentance involved. "O my God," he prayed, "I am ashamed and blush to lift up my face to thee, my God: for our iniquities are increased over our head, and our trespass is grown up unto the heavens." Ezra 9:6.

Ezra did not attempt to excuse or justify himself or his people. They had sinned. They had grieved the heart of God, they had wandered far from the great Benefactor, and the only way back, Ezra, the priest and scribe, knew was to freely admit the transgressions and in true humility "creep back to God," seeking forgiveness and pardon. For Ezra as for us today, it is either repent or perish. There is no other alternative.

After conviction *of* sin comes contrition *for* sin, which is repentance. Do *you* know the meaning of true repentance in your life?

*Sunday*

# How Sorry Are You?

When our two sons were small, they were well admonished about not eating sweets between meals. One day the younger one "forgot." His mother caught him fair and square with his hand in the cookie jar. He was sorry in a hurry, especially when he saw the switch in mother's hand. His sorrow was well expressed, but a bit late and under questionable circumstances.

So it may be with the overt sinner or the erring saint who is "caught in the act." He is sorry. He says so freely, but he may not be sorry that he has sinned, disobeyed God, and "crucified the Son of God afresh," but rather he feels bad because he has been caught, and he knows punishment is ahead.

There is a difference, the Apostle Paul declares, between grieving over inevitable punishment and sorrowing because our sin has placed the Saviour of mankind upon the cross. One is ice broken, the other is ice melted. The first—called in Scripture the sorrow of the world—fools neither God nor ourselves; the second—called godly sorrow—is our second step Godward. It is true repentance.

"For godly sorrow worketh repentance to salvation not to be repented of: but the sorrow of the world worketh death." 2 Corinthians 7:10.

Heart sorrow for sin takes us along the road that leads to life everlasting. It is incisive. It is effective. It brings about a change in our lives. The sorrow of the world—counterfeit repentance—only attempts to make our "faith" a fire escape. We don't love heaven, but we fear hell.

Have the tears trickled down *your* cheeks because *your* sins made Calvary a necessity?

*Monday*

# Setting Our House in Order

"Set thine house in order!" Isaiah 38:1. This is a stunning command in any language under any circumstances. These words were spoken by the Old Testament prophet Isaiah to King Hezekiah, who was commanded to put his house in order because he was going to die. God tells you and me to put our houses in order—not necessarily because we expect to die immediately, but rather because we have decided to live—*for Him!*

Conviction has stopped us upon our road of disobedience and sin. Contrition—repentance—has started us upon the road back to God. Our next step is *confession.* Setting our house in order involves confession, the acknowledgment of our guilt. "Take with you words, and turn to the Lord," the prophet admonishes. (Hosea 14:2.)

"When ye sin so against the brethren, and wound their weak conscience, ye sin against Christ," Paul declares. (1 Corinthians 8:12.) On the rocky road of transgression we grieve both God and man. Confession of offense to both helps us straighten things out. We confess our sins to God and our faults to those whom we have wronged.

"Make confession unto the Lord God." Ezra

10:11. There are some sins (violations of the first four commandments, and secret sins) that we need to make right with God. David recognized this when he prayed, "Against thee, thee only, have I sinned, and done this evil in thy sight." Psalm 51:4. Such sins we, too, must in humility of heart confess to God.

When we have bared our hearts before the Most High, we have the precious promise that "if we confess our sins, he is faithful and just to forgive us our sins, and to cleanse us from all unrighteousness." (1 John 1:9.)

Thus we do not have to carry around a burden of guilt when we through faith fulfill the requirements of this promise.

*Tuesday*

# It Isn't Easy, But—

We may be able to quote large portions of Scripture. We may be well versed in theology. Our church attendance may be unassailable. Our financial support of the church may be on a sacrificial basis. But if we can't get along with those around us, our Christian experience remains defective. Being on better terms with angels than with men means something is wrong with our religion.

The last six of the Ten Commandments deal with our relationships with our fellowmen. Unfortunately, on occasion, envy, bitterness, and evil surmising creep into these relationships. If we violate any of these commandments and create estrangement, then, the apostle says, "confess your faults one to another." (James 5:16.)

"I was wrong. I am sorry. Please forgive me," are some of the most difficult words to say in any language. Some people consider it a sign of weakness to use them. But when we have made mistakes, when we have wounded someone by bitter word or thoughtless action and we confess our fault to the aggrieved person, this is a sign of spiritual strength. It is proof that we are trying to pattern our life after the life of Christ.

"True confession is always of a specific character, and acknowledges particular sins. . . . [It] should be definite and to the point, acknowledging the very sins of which you are guilty."—Ellen G. White, *Steps to Christ,* p. 38.

Are there some things *you* need to make right? If so, the Apostle Paul has a word for you: "I beg you by name to make up your differences as Christians should!" Philippians 4:2, Phillips.

If you want true peace in your heart, if you would know the joy that comes with being right with God, you must also be right with those about you.

*Wednesday*

# It Takes More Than
# Window Dressing

One night Jesus was speaking to Nicodemus, a man of power and influence in Israel. To this one-man congregation the Saviour unfolded one of the most profound truths in the gospel.

"Except a man be born again, he cannot see the kingdom of God," Jesus told him. (John 3:3.) He did not say, "Unless you have been born again, it will be difficult for you to see the kingdom." He stated clearly and categorically that unless you and I have been born again in a spiritual sense, we will not see the kingdom of God.

We may have a charming personality, we may be culturally acceptable, we may be socially enviable and morally correct, but this is not enough. Our hearts, our lives, must be changed; they must be transformed before we are fit for the kingdom of heaven.

Both Jesus and Paul reveal why this must be so: "The carnal mind is enmity against God." Romans 8:7. "Out of the heart proceed evil thoughts, murders, adulteries, fornications, thefts, false witness, blasphemies." Matthew 15:19.

Just a little retouching of the old life, a bit of window dressing, an acceptable outward veneer, is not enough. There must be a complete change. The old heart and life must be replaced. Nothing short of a new birth will suffice. We can't go into the kingdom with a perfect God, with perfect angels, and with perfect saints if we retain our old propensities to evil. We must be entirely new creatures. (2 Corinthians 5:17.)

The Spirit of God effects this transformation. He makes us over after the likeness of our Saviour. He breaks our hard hearts, and a new life, built upon the new covenant, replaces the old.

*Thursday*

# How Can I Be Sure?

Our encounter with Christ in the experience of conversion, or the new birth, may be cataclysmic, as it was with the Apostle Paul on the way to Damascus. You, too, may experience some violent emotion, some great upheaval in your life, when Jesus leads you to the point of surrender.

On the other hand, it is quite likely that yours may be a less dramatic, less traumatic, experience. In fact, you may not be able to tell the exact time and place that the all-important event of conversion

occurred. Little by little, perhaps almost unconsciously, the impressions were made which led you
to break with sin and to ally yourself with your Saviour. Whether sudden and startling, or gradual and
unspectacular, conversion must come, but it is just
as real in either case.

How may you know that you have experienced
conversion, which is also referred to as the new
birth? Jesus answers the question for you: "Wherefore by their fruits ye shall know them." Matthew
7:20.

Our new experience will become evident in life
service more than in lip service. We will not need
to tell others—they will *know* that something very
important has taken place in our lives. Our families
will know it. Our friends will know it. Those with
whom we work will discover it. Even the dog and
cat around the house will be aware of it. True conversion is not something that can be hidden, nor is it
something we need to tell others about. They will immediately recognize what has happened in our lives.

Where we go, whom we go with, what we see,
what we hear, what we say, will reveal that the
power of God has been at work in our lives. Not
only our thoughts, but our actions and deeds change.

How does the experience come? We decide to
place our lives in Christ's hands and yield our ways
to Him to be guided by His Holy Spirit.

*Friday*

# How Faith Works

Often we think of the eleventh chapter of the Book of Hebrews as the great faith chapter of the Bible. It is largely devoted to examples of faith exhibited in the lives of some of the best-known Biblical characters. But the eighth chapter of Matthew also contains accounts of outstanding examples of faith.

See the measure of trust shown by the poor leper: "When he was come down from the mountain, great multitudes followed him. And, behold, there came a leper and worshipped him, saying, Lord, if thou wilt, thou canst make me clean. And Jesus put forth his hand, and touched him, saying, I will; be thou clean. And immediately his leprosy was cleansed." Matthew 8:2, 3.

The leper's faith brought him cleansing of body —perhaps also of soul.

Even among the Romans, whom the Jews despised as occupation troops representing an alien culture, there were commendable examples of faith, as this passage from Matthew shows: "And when Jesus was entered into Capernaum, there came unto him a centurion, beseeching him, and saying, Lord, my servant lieth at home sick of the palsy, grievously tormented. And Jesus saith unto him, I will come and heal him. The centurion answered and said, Lord, I am not worthy that thou shouldest come under my roof: but speak the word only, and my servant shall be healed." Matthew 8:5-8.

The centurion's faith brought healing for his trusted servant, and this word of commendation from the Master, "I have not found so great faith, no, not in Israel." Verse 10.

Peter's sick mother-in-law must have had a considerable measure of faith, for when Jesus touched her, "she arose, and ministered unto them." (Verse 15.)

If we are to receive the blessing of God, we must have faith also. Like the leper, the centurion, and Peter's mother-in-law, we must trust God implicitly.

We must learn to pray, "Lord, increase our faith."

*Saturday*

# Why Prayers Are Not Answered

You have prayed many times and God has not answered? Then there must be something drastically wrong. Christ said, "Ask, and it shall be given you; seek, and ye shall find; knock, and it shall be opened unto you." Matthew 7:7.

Now let's think this matter through carefully. Could it be that you have not met the requirements of Heaven for answered prayer? There are several of these requirements.

First, we must exercise faith. The Scriptures state, "What things soever ye desire, when ye pray, believe that ye receive them, and ye shall have them." Mark 11:24. "But without faith it is impossible to please him: for he that cometh to God must believe that he is, and that he is a rewarder of them that diligently seek him." Hebrews 11:6.

A second requirement is that we be clean spiritually. David wrote, "If I regard iniquity in my heart, the Lord will not hear me." Psalm 66:18. Sin separates us from God. "Behold, the Lord's hand is not shortened, that it cannot save; neither his ear heavy, that it cannot hear: but your iniquities have separated between you and your God, and your sins have hid his face from you, that he will not hear." Isaiah 59:1, 2.

A third and extremely important condition is that we are to ask according to God's will. He can see the end from the beginning. "Remember the former things of old: for I am God, and there is none else; I am God, and there is none like me, declaring the end from the beginning, and from ancient times the things that are not yet done, saying, My counsel shall stand, and I will do all my pleasure." Isaiah 46:9, 10. He knows what is best for us, and He will permit only what is for our best good. "He that spared not his own Son, but delivered him up for us all, how shall he not with him also freely give us all things?" Romans 8:32.

A fourth requirement is that in seeking the Lord's guidance and help we be ready to respond in harmony with His counsel. We cannot expect Him to shower His blessings upon those who willfully ignore Him; for "he that turneth away his ear from hearing the law, even his prayer shall be abomination." (Proverbs 28:9.) If we walk obediently in His way, we need have no fear, "and whatsoever we ask, we receive of him, because we keep his commandments, and do those things that are pleasing in his sight." (1 John 3:22.) These requirements are perfectly understandable. In human relations we often stipulate certain standards before we consider a person worthy of certain kinds of aid or responsibilities. God knows that man must meet certain standards to best use answered prayer.

Have your prayers not been answered? Perhaps there is some reason why God has not answered your prayers. If you meet the requirements, God will do His part in keeping the promise that "every one that asketh receiveth; and he that seeketh findeth; and to him that knocketh it shall be opened." (Matthew 7:8.)

*Sunday*

# What Shall We Pray For?

What exactly should we pray for? Among the things we perhaps need most are forgiveness of sin and spiritual cleansing. God promises both to us: "If we confess our sins, he is faithful and just to forgive us our sins, and to cleanse us from all unrighteousness." 1 John 1:9. "Come now, and let us reason together, saith the Lord: though your sins be as scarlet, they shall be as white as snow; though they be red like crimson, they shall be as wool." Isaiah 1:18.

We may need to pray also for wisdom to understand God's will. "If any of you lack wisdom, let him ask of God, that giveth to all men liberally, and upbraideth not; and it shall be given him." James 1:5.

We may pray for our temporal needs, our daily bread. God knows His children need food to eat, clothes to wear, a place to stay, and He will supply these things when we ask of Him, "Give us this day our daily bread." Matthew 6:11. The psalmist was confident that God hears the cry of the needy. He wrote, "I have been young, and now am old; yet have I not seen the righteous forsaken, nor his seed begging bread." Psalm 37:25.

We should pray for the sick. Many a man has walked away from a deathbed when the power of God flooded his life with healing as a result of prayer. The Apostle James tells us, "The prayer of faith shall save the sick, and the Lord shall raise him up; and if he have committed sins, they shall be forgiven him." James 5:15.

We may pray for protection. The promises of the ninety-first Psalm are as certain of fulfillment today as they were at the time the psalmist wrote them: "He that dwelleth in the secret place of the most High shall abide under the shadow of the Almighty. I will say of the Lord, He is my refuge and my fortress: my God; in him will I trust." Psalm 91: 1, 2.

We should pray for the spiritual needs of those whom we know need help. "Pray one for another," the Apostle James says, for "the effectual fervent prayer of a righteous man availeth much." (James 5:16.)

We should pray for our friends, for by doing so we can help them and receive a blessing ourselves, as Job discovered. "The Lord turned the captivity of Job, when he prayed for his friends." Job 42:10.

The leaders of government need our support and prayers. "Let every soul be subject unto the higher powers. For there is no power but of God: the powers that be are ordained of God." Romans 13:1.

In these days of turmoil, how much the rulers of the nations need our prayers!

We should pray for the discouraged people all around us, even though we may not know them. God will answer our prayers when we offer them for strangers as well as when we offer them for ourselves. Christ said, "And all things, whatsoever ye shall ask in prayer, believing, ye shall receive." Matthew 21:22.

*Monday*

# We Can Know God

As human beings, we have the privilege of becoming personally acquainted with God. How do we do this? Ellen G. White has beautifully written about how this relationship develops between God and man:

"Through nature and revelation, through His providence, and by the influence of His Spirit, God speaks to us. But these are not enough; we need also to pour out our hearts to Him. In order to have spiritual life and energy, we must have actual intercourse with our heavenly Father. Our minds may be drawn out toward Him; we may meditate upon His works, His mercies, His blessings; but this is not, in the fullest sense, communing with Him. In order to commune with God, we must have something to say to Him concerning our actual life.

"Prayer is the opening of the heart to God as to a friend. Not that it is necessary in order to make known to God what we are, but in order to enable us to receive Him. Prayer does not bring God down to us, but brings us up to Him.

"When Jesus was upon the earth, He taught His disciples how to pray. He directed them to present their daily needs before God, and to cast all their care upon Him. And the assurance He gave them that their petitions should be heard, is assurance also to us.

"Jesus Himself, while He dwelt among men, was often in prayer. Our Saviour identified Himself with our needs and weakness, in that He became a suppliant, a petitioner, seeking from His Father fresh supplies of strength, that He might come forth braced for duty and trial. He is our example in all things. He is a brother in our infirmities, 'in all points tempted like as we are;' but as the sinless one His nature recoiled from evil; He endured struggles and torture of soul in a world of sin. His humanity made prayer a necessity and a privilege. He found comfort and joy in communion with His Father. And if the Saviour of men . . . felt the need of prayer, how much more should feeble, sinful mortals feel the necessity of fervent, constant prayer.

"Our heavenly Father waits to bestow upon us the fullness of His blessing. It is our privilege to drink largely at the fountain of boundless love. What a wonder it is that we pray so little! God is ready and willing to hear the sincere prayer of the humblest of His children, and yet there is much manifest reluctance on our part to make known our wants to God. What can the angels of heaven think of poor helpless human beings, who are subject to temptation, when God's heart of infinite love yearns toward them, ready to give them more than they can ask or think, and yet they pray so little and have so little faith? The angels love to bow before God; they love to be near Him. They regard communion with God as their highest joy; and yet the children of earth, who need so much the help that God only can give, seem satisfied to walk without the light of His Spirit, the companionship of His presence."—*Steps to Christ,* pp. 93, 94.

*Tuesday*

# Living a Perfect Life

David uttered a universal human desire when in one of his Psalms he cried to God, "Create in me a clean heart, O God; and renew a right spirit within me. Cast me not away from thy presence; and take not thy holy spirit from me. Restore unto me the joy of thy salvation; and uphold me with thy free spirit." Psalm 51:10-12.

In his remarkable prayer of repentance David sets forth six requirements for living a perfect Christian life:

1. *"Create in me a clean heart."* God begins with our heart. Before He can do anything with the rest of our being, our heart must be clean. The Christian life. begins with a renewed heart—the new birth.

2. *"Renew a right spirit within me."* A Christian living in the presence of God will maintain attitudes of kindness toward his fellowmen. His will be a loving, forgiving spirit. If such a spirit is not ours, we need to examine ourselves and with God's help develop a right spirit toward others.

3. *"Cast me not away from thy presence."* An "abiding Christian" dwells in the presence of God. When our words, thoughts, and actions can bear the test of the Saviour's presence, we are beginning to achieve perfection.

4. *"Take not thy holy spirit from me."* The Holy Spirit acts as a refining influence on the Christian and enables him to live in harmony with God and man. Prayer is essential in retaining the Holy Spirit.

5. *"Restore unto me the joy of thy salvation."* Real Christianity fills the heart with joy. All whose lives touch ours will be inspired by our happy,

wholesome outlook on life. Joy is very infectious.

6. *"Uphold me with thy free spirit."* Victory in Christian living comes only through the power of God, and if we, as did David, call upon God, He will give us victory in our lives.

*Wednesday*

# Is There an "Instant Religion"?

Store shelves are groaning under the weight of foods and drinks which can be prepared instantly—instant milk, instant chocolate, instant coffee, instant Postum, instant potatoes, instant waffles, instant puddings, and instant what-have-you. We live in a maddeningly busy age, and Americans are among the busiest of people. We rush around; we dash in and out. We impatiently honk our horns when the traffic light turns amber, fearful lest the driver ahead waste a split second of our precious time. Often as not, however, we hurry up to wait; and many times we are impatient to rush somewhere in order to participate in nothing more than trivia.

Americans are great travelers. We swarm through Europe, crowd hotels, and choke beaches in the West Indies. We gape at marvelous antiquities in the Middle East and spill over into the more exotic lands of the Orient. A few of us hurry home to write books, publish articles, or verbally impart words of wisdom as "experts" on the lands we have visited. But too many of us are tourists, instead of experts, even when it comes to things that really matter.

Some people even want their religion to be served instantly. But perhaps God should slow some of us down a bit—and put a Bible in our hands for more than a few fleeting glances at a time.

There is tremendous power in these words from the Bible: "Be still, and know that I am God." God seeks to slow our steps, so that we can indeed know Him and ourselves better.

Instead of instant religion we need constant religion. We need not only Bibles in our hands, we desperately need Bibles in our hearts and in our lives. This will become blessed reality only when you and I heed Paul's instruction, "Study to shew thyself approved unto God." 2 Timothy 2:15.

*Thursday*

# You May Be Starving to Death

How much food do you consume in one year? According to an estimate of the United States Department of Agriculture, the average American consumes 1,488 pounds of food annually. That is a lot

of potatoes, pies, and ice cream. Little wonder many
of us need to watch our calories, or we will be watching our waistlines.

But does "eating well" bring health? Jesus has
something to say about our diet, and we would do
well to consider His words carefully and prayerfully.
Jesus said, "It is written, Man shall not live by bread
alone, but by every word that proceedeth out of the
mouth of God." Matthew 4:4.

Feeding the body is essential, but feeding the
soul is even more important if we wish to grow
spiritually. A person will soon starve to death if he
stops eating physical food. He will soon die spiritually if he fails to feed amply on the Bread of Life—
the Holy Scriptures. Lack of physical food will cause
physical death. Lack of spiritual food—the Bible—
will cause eternal spiritual death.

Billy Graham said, "You would not expect to
lead a healthy physical life unless you ate your meals
regularly. Show the same amount of common sense
about preserving your spiritual life in a vigorous and
healthy state. Daily Bible reading is an essential part
of our spiritual diet."

"Every word of God is pure," the Scriptures tell
us. If we feed our minds on that which is cheap and
evil, we cannot hope to become spiritually robust.
We cannot live by bread alone. Both the body and
the mind need many kinds of nutrients. Our suste-

nance must derive from "every word that proceedeth out of the mouth of God."

Many people are literally starving themselves to death spiritually by failure to feed on the Word of God. We need God's Word in our daily quest for happiness. Without it, we will fail.

# SECTION V

# A Solution for Man's Problems

Less than a block ahead the raging, howling mob was looting shops and destroying property. Police stopped my friend and me just in time for us to turn around and get out of the troubled area. The place was Bombay, India. The cause of the uproar was another Hindu-Muslim religious squabble, during which scores of people were killed and widespread damage was done. For centuries such religious hatred has sparked bloodshed and vandalism.

Several times I have visited the Middle East, the birthplace of three great religions—Judaism, Christianity, and Islam. For centuries this area has been the scene of strife. The problems that separate Jew and Arab have thus far defied solution.

At least thirty newly independent African nations have burst upon the scene of action during the past few years. But deep tribal animosities keep the political pots boiling in many of these lands. The fires of hatred smolder or periodically burst into flame across the continent.

The giants of East and West—Russia and America and their satellites and allies—glare and plot or fight on many fronts across the world. Who can heal the wounds of Korea, Vietnam, Berlin, or scores of other sensitive areas?

In fact, what statesman or group of statesmen can satisfactorily or permanently settle the myriad problems of our world? None who can do so are on the horizon today. The wounds are too deep, disillusionment too universal, the destruction of faith too complete. It is midnight in the history of the world, and man cannot resolve his problems. Only divine deliverance will suffice. Thank God, it is promised —a Deliverer will come.

"For yet a little while, and he that shall come will come, and will not tarry." Hebrews 10:37.

*Saturday*

# A Promise to Be Kept

"I shall return!" How those courageous words spoken by Gen. Douglas MacArthur buoyed the hopes of many in the Philippines during the long years of enemy occupation. What a moment of fulfillment it was when the returning general and his troops waded ashore on the island of Leyte years later to begin the bloody task of liberation.

Several of my friends were interned in Los Banos prison near Manila during World War II when American paratroopers floated down from low-flying planes to cooperate with ground forces in releasing 2,156 men and women who had been held as civilian internees for forty-two months. What a glorious day of deliverance this was for these prisoners! The long nightmare of fear and famine was ended. The feelings of joy that coursed through their minds, the tears that wet their eyes and streamed down their faces, the strange sense of sudden freedom—none of these things would the prisoners soon forget.

Today another Deliverer is due. One greater than any earthly general has promised deliverance from a world filled with heartaches, pain, and death. Nearly two thousand years ago that Deliverer promised, "I go to prepare a place for you. And if I go and prepare a place for you, *I will come again,* and receive you unto myself; that where I am, there ye may be also." John 14:2, 3.

"*If I go, . . .* I will come again," Jesus promised. His departure is a recorded fact: "And when he had spoken these things, while they beheld, he was taken up; and a cloud received him out of their sight." Acts 1:9. That He will come back can be believed as readily as the fact that He went away. He made His promise not as a man, but as God.

Jesus left a world in bondage, but He is coming back on a great mission of deliverance. Our Great Comforter will keep His promise to return.

*Sunday*

# Old Testament References to Christ's Second Coming

Soon after the dawn of civilization, Old Testament prophets began speaking of Christ's glorious second advent. "And Enoch also, the seventh from Adam, prophesied of these, saying, Behold, the Lord cometh with ten thousands of his saints." Jude 14.

This same precious assurance sustained Job during his days of affliction fifteen hundred years before Christ. "For I know that my redeemer liveth, and that he shall stand at the latter day upon the earth: and though after my skin worms destroy this body, yet in my flesh shall I see God." Job 19:25, 26.

The psalmist was inspired to describe the glory of Christ's return: "Our God shall come, and shall not keep silence: a fire shall devour before him, and it shall be very tempestuous round about him. He shall call to the heavens from above, and to the earth, that he may judge his people. Gather my saints together unto me; those that have made a covenant with me by sacrifice." Psalm 50:3-5.

The prophet Isaiah visualized the splendor of the return of Christ: "For, behold, the Lord will come with fire, and with his chariots like a whirlwind, to render his anger with fury, and his rebuke with flames of fire. For by fire and by his sword will the Lord plead with all flesh: and the slain of the Lord shall be many." Isaiah 66:15, 16.

Jeremiah, Daniel, Joel, Zephaniah, Haggai, Malachi, and other Old Testament writers believed in and wrote concerning the glorious second coming. Through the centuries this blessed hope has sustained prophets and kings, priests and laymen, alike.

*Monday*

# New Testament References to Christ's Second Coming

"I will come again." (See John 14:1-3.) The New Testament rings with this promise of Jesus, for it is mentioned 318 times in 260 chapters—an average of one verse in every twenty-five.

While under oath before Caiaphas, the Jewish high priest, Jesus gave assurance of His return: "I say unto you, Hereafter shall ye see the Son of man sitting on the right hand of power, and coming in the clouds of heaven." Matthew 26:64.

Angels promised the sorrowing disciples that their Master would return to earth: "And while they looked stedfastly toward heaven as he went up, behold, two men stood by them in white apparel; which also said, Ye men of Galilee, why stand ye gazing up into heaven? this same Jesus, which is taken up from you into heaven, shall so come in like manner as ye have seen him go into heaven." Acts 1:10, 11.

The Apostle Paul, writing to young Titus, described the second advent as a glorious event to which we should look forward in glad anticipation: "Looking for that blessed hope, and the glorious appearing of the great God and our Saviour Jesus Christ." Titus 2:13.

Peter mentions the rewards to be given to those who are prepared when Jesus returns: "And when the chief Shepherd shall appear, ye shall receive a crown of glory that fadeth not away." 1 Peter 5:4.

Through the words of the Book of Revelation, Jesus (Revelation 1:1), in the closing verses of inspired Scripture, leaves this promise: "And, behold, I come quickly; and my reward is with me, to give every man according as his work shall be." Revelation 22:12. God's promises are not ambiguous. No one can argue that the Bible doesn't give enough evidence to judge whether He will return or not. The promises are clear, unmistakable.

What precious assurances—Jesus is coming again.

*Tuesday*

# Signs of Christ's Coming

A few years ago in the northern part of the Belgian Congo we had car trouble, and I waited in a little park on the shore of Lake Albert while the repairs were made. The government administrator of a large nearby district happened along, and soon we chatted as amiably as his broken English and my thirty-word French vocabulary permitted.

The conversation turned to world events, and I referred to the prophecies of the Bible and stated that the dangers of war and the unrest and trouble hanging over many parts of the world seemed to be a fulfillment of Christ's words describing conditions just before His second coming.

"But," my friend objected good-naturedly, "there have always been wars and threats of war—all down through history."

"Yes," I said, "what you say is true, but never has the world known war and political violence on anything like the scale we are witnessing in our day." Then I refreshed his memory with some facts of history in many lands in recent years. He readily agreed that no previous generation had experienced turmoil and trouble on the scale our tortured generation has experienced it.

The same objection my Belgian friend made was urged in the Apostle Peter's day: "Where is the promise of his coming? for since the fathers fell asleep, all things continue as they were from the beginning of the creation." 2 Peter 3:4.

Peter reminds us that doubters and scoffers are themselves signposts announcing the soon return of Jesus: "There shall come in the last days scoffers" who will challenge the truth of the advent. (Verse 3.) He also mentions that they "willingly are ignorant." (Verse 5.) Let us not let this day come upon us as a "thief in the night." (Verse 10.) Seeing we "know these things" (verse 17), let us watch and be ready. Sometimes we can remedy the problems that result when we are late—but not this time.

*Wednesday*

# "I Love Violence"

"I love violence," the leader of a Los Angeles activist group stated in his opening remarks at an extremist conference in Newark, New Jersey. This man must have been elated with what his eyes beheld across America in the summer of 1967. From Watts to Wichita, to Waterloo, to Wilmington, American cities spewed violence in all directions.

Rock throwing, fire-bombing, looting, gunfire, snip-
ing, the sounds of death, hatred, and resentment
were the order of the day in the Negro areas of
many American cities.

Headlines across the nation shrieked the same
sad story: "Gun Battles Break Out," "Guardsmen
Shoot, People Loot," "Guerrilla Warfare Flares in
City," "March! Maryland Rioters Urged."

Detroit became the scene of the costliest and
the bloodiest uprising in half a century. In a single
week more than forty people were killed, hundreds
were injured. Thousands were arrested. Thousands
more were homeless. More than 3,000 buildings
were razed by fire, 2,700 businesses were sacked
and gutted. Hundreds of millions of dollars' worth
of property was damaged during the uprising. "Violence is necessary. It is as American as cherry pie,"
one radical leader admonished a crowd.

After Detroit, the President of the United States
said sadly, "We have endured a week such as no
nation should live through: a time of violence and
tragedy."—*Time,* August 4, 1967.

The late Senator Robert F. Kennedy described
the situation in mid-1967 as "the greatest domestic
crisis since the War Between the States." A foreign
correspondent said, "The outbreak has become
something more than a race riot."

"The last days," Paul writes, "will be full of

danger." 2 Timothy 3:1, Phillips. The prophet Jeremiah saw that the cities of earth "shall be laid waste." (Jeremiah 4:7.) We dare not fail to catch the significance of violence in the cities. God's voice is seeking to arouse a spiritually indifferent world to a realization of the times in which we live. The second coming of Christ is near at hand.

*Thursday*

# Bombs or Babies?

In one nation where government officials estimate that between four hundred thousand and one million people may starve in a single year, a toothless old woman lay on a nest of rags in her dirty hovel.

"My daughter has gone to beg," she told an inquiring newsman, "and my son has gone to look for work. It has been months since we had a full meal. How do I know that either my son or daughter will bring me food tonight?"

In the same village an eighteen-year-old boy, slowly starving to death, lamented weakly, "I don't remember when I last ate."

Statisticians are now saying that during the next decade over a billion people—yes, a *billion* people —may die of hunger. Lester Brown, Economic Research Service, United States Department of Agriculture, declares that "hunger will be the world's number one problem in the days ahead—famine looms as a prospect that can become more serious than the threat of nuclear war."

The world's population is increasing at the rate of one hundred million babies a year. Even though half that number may die, it still means an annual increase of some fifty million stomachs to be filled.

It took from the beginning of the human race until the year 1830 for one billion people to be alive on the earth at one time. But the population jumped to two billion in just one century—1830-1930. By 1961, less than a third of a century later, it had climbed to three billion. At this rate, in less than a decade the world's population will be four billion, and before the end of this century it will have reached six billion.

Where will sufficient food come from to feed these billions of hungry mouths?

America will be unable to play the leading role she now plays. "By 1985 the world will have to find another breadbasket besides ours," a recent advertisement declares. "That's the year when the food needs of the world's underdeveloped nations will be so great it will be impossible for this country to meet them." According to the United States Department of Agriculture, even if we put every single one of

America's now idle fifty-five million acres of land into full production, we will fall short of required food production by about twelve million tons.

There are lean, hungry days ahead for millions of earth's underfed, days of famine and death. What does all this mean? Jesus Himself declared that "famines, and pestilences . . . in divers places" will be yet another sign of His "coming, and of the end of the world." (Matthew 24:7, 3.)

*Friday*

# From Muscles to Missiles

Speed of transportation is a fairly safe index of technological advance. Some four thousand years after the birth of the human family, man could travel only as fast as a horse could pull or carry him. Even fifteen centuries later rich and poor alike were dependent upon the horse for transportation.

Not until 1830, when the steam locomotive was invented, was man able to travel faster than the horse, but only eighty years after that, the first contract for the production of military planes was let. The contract agreement provided that 10 percent of the stipulated price would be deducted for each mile the plane fell short of forty miles an hour. The manufacturers, however, produced a plane which performed at a top speed of forty-two miles an hour.

Toward the end of World War I, fighter planes were flying 150 miles an hour. At the outbreak of World War II, planes were flying up to 200 miles an hour, and doubled their speed by the war's end.

Then suddenly technologists were making more progress in a week than they had previously made in a year. Men blasted through the sound barrier. Then came the Sputniks, the Explorers, the Vanguards, the Luniks, and a host of other satellites.

"In recent years astrophysicists have opened up the gates of heaven," says W. R. Beach, "while the nuclear physicists have opened the gates of hell."

Technology has gone from muscles to missiles in an amazingly short time. The Old Testament prophet Daniel, writing about "the time of the end," stated that "many shall run to and fro, and knowledge shall be increased." (Daniel 12:4.)

*Saturday*

# Hope in Heaven

The thought that Christ is soon to return should bring joy to every Christian's heart. Think what it would mean if today the cry went forth, "Christ is come!" What relief from pain and suffering this would mean to millions of patients in hospitals and nursing homes, for when Jesus comes, "neither shall there be any more pain." (Revelation 21:4.) No more headaches or backaches, no more twisted limbs or fevered brows. There will be no more need for hospitals when Jesus comes, for He is our Great Physician as well as our all-sufficient Saviour.

When the cry goes forth, "Christ is come," there will be no more death for God's loved ones, no more lonely vigils by the side of a beloved mother or father, son or daughter, watching them take their last halting breaths. Then "God shall wipe away all tears from their eyes; and there shall be no more death, neither sorrow, nor crying" in the blessed day when Jesus comes as man's great Life-giver!

When Christ returns, all problems of government, of society, of religion, will be forever settled. There will be no more bloodshed or warfare, no more poverty or despair, no more riots, no more hunger, no more loneliness or discouragement. When Jesus comes, all of the world's ills will be forever settled.

Little wonder that pain-racked saints and heart-broken believers have long prayed earnestly, "Even so, come, Lord Jesus." Revelation 22:20. Little wonder the Apostle Paul says that all saints should be "looking for *that blessed hope,* and the glorious appearing of the great God and our Saviour Jesus Christ." (Titus 2:13.)

*Sunday*

# The Prints of the Nails

Some years ago an old man with a beaming smile and kindly ways walked the streets of Los Angeles. "I am Jesus Christ," he said as he placed his hands on the heads of little children. "I have returned to claim my people as my own."

As crowds gathered about the white-haired old gentleman, a Salvation Army worker on a corner across the street was singing, "I shall know Him by the prints of the nails in His hands."

"Where are the prints of the nails in *your* hands? Let us see them!" hecklers demanded of the professed Messiah. "If you are truly Jesus, you will have the marks!"

In shame the old impostor fled down a nearby alley.

When Christ returns the second time, we may know of a certainty that it is He. There need be no deception. Note this inspired account of His ascension:

"And while they looked stedfastly toward heaven as he went up, behold, two men stood by them in white apparel; which also said, Ye men of Galilee, why stand ye gazing up into heaven? this same Jesus, which is taken up from you into heaven, shall so come in like manner as ye have seen him go into heaven." Acts 1:10, 11.

"This same Jesus"—the same flesh-and-blood Jesus who walked the dusty roads of Galilee. The same Jesus who brought comfort to broken hearts, who gave hope to the hopeless, who helped all who were in need. The same Jesus who healed the sick, raised the dead, and cast out devils. The same Jesus who went to the cross for you, for me. The Jesus with the prints of the nails in His hands is the Jesus who is coming back a second time.

*Monday*

# Pews or Playhouse?

Recently a friend of mine visited one of the famous cathedrals in Europe. As he entered, a priest approached him. "Are you a tourist?" the clergyman inquired. When my friend said Yes, the priest said, "There is a religious service in progress. Would you care to come in?"

The priest led him into the twilight of the cavernous edifice and seated him near the front. After a moment of silent prayer my friend looked up, his eyes becoming accustomed to the semidarkness. He seemed to be alone. Then he heard a voice reading in a half-chanting monotone. Straining his eyes, he saw a priest in the high pulpit. When the reading was finished, the minister sat down. From the twilight of the choir loft came the voices of a small choir. The choral number faded away, and all was quiet. Then the priest and the members of the choir filed quickly out.

My friend looked around, expecting to see other worshipers in the huge cathedral. Then he realized he was entirely alone. Had he not entered, the formal service would have been conducted before empty pews. The fire in the hearts of the cathedral members evidently had long since gone out.

Today the amusement parks, the theaters, and the entertainment halls are full, but too many churches are nearly empty. What does this mean? The Apostle Paul says, "This know also, that in *the last days* . . . men shall be . . . lovers of pleasures more than lovers of God; having a form of godliness, but denying the power thereof." 2 Timothy 3: 1-5. It means that we are in *the last days*.

*Tuesday*

# Where Do You Want to Live?

In some nations today one dares not preach about the soon coming of Christ. Such philosophy does not fit the plans of ambitious statesmen absorbed with a godless ideology. In one such country a minister whom I know served three years in prison for disregarding a dictum against such preaching.

The idea that Jesus is coming soon didn't fit the thinking of Ruby, a little girl in the mission field. After six years away from home, Ruby's father and mother were preparing to return on furlough to their homeland. For weeks Ruby looked forward to the thrilling experience of returning to the fabulous land of her birth. Then one day as her parents were talking about the soon coming of Jesus, Ruby's little face grew serious.

"I don't want Jesus to come now," she sobbed. "I want to go on furlough!" Then, noting the distressed look on her parents' faces, Ruby added brightly, "But when we get back from America, I want Jesus to come!"

Yes, the thought of Christ's return does not always fit into our thinking or planning. An ancient king once had such an experience.

About six hundred years before Christ was born, Nebuchadnezzar, king of Babylon, had a dream; but when he awoke, he was unable to remember what the dream was about. He called for his magicians, his astrologers, and his sorcerers to tell him what he had dreamed and what the strange dream meant. None of them could help.

A young man named Daniel, who worshiped the

The deserted church symbolized the emptiness
of some modern-day Christianity.

living God, finally was called, and with divine help disclosed the dream to the Babylonian monarch.

"Thou, O king, sawest, and behold a great image . . . whose brightness was excellent, . . . and the form . . . was terrible. This image's head was of fine gold, his breast and his arms of silver, his belly and his thighs of brass, his legs of iron, his feet part of iron and part of clay. . . . A stone was cut out without hands, which smote the image upon his feet . . . and brake them to pieces. Then was the iron, the clay, the brass, the silver, and the gold, broken to pieces together, and became like the chaff of the summer threshingfloors, and the wind carried them away: . . . and the stone . . . became a great mountain, and filled the whole earth." Daniel 2: 31-35.

How does the interpretation of this wonderful dream affect you?

*Wednesday*

# History Before It Happens

Here is the interpretation of King Nebuchadnezzar's dream as Daniel gave it: "Thou, O king, . . . art this head of gold. And after thee shall arise another kingdom inferior to thee, and another third kingdom of brass, which shall bear rule over all the earth. And the fourth kingdom shall be strong as iron. . . . And whereas thou sawest the feet and toes, part of potters' clay, and part of iron, the kingdom shall be divided. . . . And as the toes of the feet were part of iron, and part of clay, so the kingdom shall be partly strong, and partly broken." Daniel 2: 37-42.

Nebuchadnezzar and Daniel were given the rare privilege of viewing the rise and fall of nations then unknown. Inspired writers and authors of history have recorded the fulfillment of Nebuchadnezzar's dream. In due time Medo-Persia, the silver kingdom, seized the scepter from golden Babylon's reigning monarch, Belshazzar. Greece, represented by the belly and thighs of brass, under Alexander the Great, conquered Medo-Persia and much of the ancient world. Then iron Rome under the Caesars broke the power of Greece and became the ruler of the world.

Weakened by internal corruption, Rome, too, came to its end. The empire was broken into ten divisions—the Anglo-Saxons, the Franks, the Alemanni, the Lombards, the Ostrogoths, the Visigoths, the Burgundians, the Vandals, the Suevi, and the Heruli. Even in the nations of modern Europe seven of these divisions are easily traceable. The prophecy of God's Word has been unerringly fulfilled in every detail.

*Thursday*

# Another World Ruler?

"And whereas thou sawest iron mixed with miry clay, they shall mingle themselves with the seed of men: but they shall not cleave one to another, even as iron is not mixed with clay." Daniel 2:43.

In the interpretation of the dream, Nebuchadnezzar was shown a prolonged and determined attempt to weld the nations of Western Europe together into one great European supernation. He was also shown by divine revelation that these attempts would never be successful. Just as iron and clay will not mix, just so the various nations of Europe seem incapable of joining together, for as the prophetic dream interpretation states, *"They shall not cleave one to another."* Charlemagne, Charles V, Louis XIV, Napoleon, Kaiser Wilhelm, Adolf Hitler, all tried their hands at total European conquest. Some almost succeeded, but in the end, God's Word stood. *"They shall not cleave one to another."* Those seven words will defeat the ambitions of any power-hungry dictator in the future, just as they have stood for centuries in the past. The nations of Europe will never again become one great superpower. God's Word declares it. History's record since the fall of Rome discourages any such attempt.

But another world ruler will arise "in the days of these kings."

"And in the days of these kings shall the God of heaven set up a kingdom, which shall never be destroyed." Daniel 2:44.

Nebuchadnezzar and Daniel gazed at last upon a kingdom that shall know no end, one which will be established when Christ returns as King of kings and Lord of lords. The Prince of peace at His second advent will "set up a kingdom, which shall never be destroyed."

What a blessed assurance! There can be no doubt about it. God says "the dream is *certain*, and the interpretation thereof *sure*." (Daniel 2:45.)

We need not base our hope upon the shifting sands of man's predictions. The eternal God speaks. The One who knows the end from the beginning unfolds the future to those who will look and study. Christ's coming is certain. The interpretation of the dream is sure.

*Friday*

# Why a Second Coming?

Why a second coming? Have you ever attended a family reunion when all the children came to be with the old folks? Many weeks go into excited planning for the event, especially on the part of dad and mother.

Christ loves His earthbound children. He wants them with Him. "Where I am," He promises, "there ye may be also." He is looking forward to His family's great reunion day. He has gone to prepare a place for us, and He has promised that He will come again to take us to be with Him always. (John 14:3.)

Loved ones who have gone to sleep in death will be raised from their dusty beds on the first resurrection morning at Christ's second coming. "The Lord himself shall descend from heaven with a shout, with the voice of the archangel, and with the trump of God: and the dead in Christ shall rise first." 1 Thessalonians 4:16.

Those who live to see the Saviour without suffering death will "be caught up together with them in the clouds, to meet the Lord in the air." (Verse 17.) Loved ones long separated will be united, nevermore to part.

The second advent is the climax of the plan of redemption—the time when the Saviour will come to claim His own out of a world of sin. "They shall be mine, saith the Lord of hosts, in that day when I make up my jewels." Malachi 3:17.

There will be no more separations for "so shall we ever be with the Lord." (1 Thessalonians 4:17.)

*Saturday*

# The Greatest News Event

The words of Scripture, "This same Jesus," clearly describe the manner in which Christ will return to earth. The disciples and many others *saw* Jesus ascend into heaven. The angels announced that He would return the same way. (Acts 1:11.) Jesus confirmed that His second advent would be a *visible* return. In Luke 21:27 He is quoted as saying, "Then shall they see the Son of man coming in a cloud with power and great glory."

Christ Himself makes clear that His coming will be no secret: "Wherefore if they shall say unto you, Behold, he is in the desert; go not forth: behold, he is in the secret chambers; believe it not. For as the lightning cometh out of the east, and shineth even unto the west; so shall also the coming of the Son of man be." Matthew 24:26, 27. As visible as the flash of lightning streaking across the midnight sky will be the return of our Lord.

"Behold, he cometh with clouds; and every eye shall see him, and they also which pierced him." Revelation 1:7. Righteous and wicked alike, *every eye* will behold a returning Lord!

Your eyes, my eyes, the eyes of every human being, will behold the Saviour face to face in that

great day. Will it be a thrilling, joyous occasion for
you, or will it be a day of darkness and fear? Our
relationship to Him now determines how we greet
Him when He returns. If we love Him now, we will
meet Him joyously then.

*Sunday*

# Be "Always Ready"

The town of South Shields on the north coast of
England has as its motto, "Always Ready." The
words appear on a shield with a lifeboat on the
community's coat of arms. South Shields was the
first English town to inaugurate the plan of having
lifeboats on the coast to help those in need.

For every Christian who is looking for the soon
coming of Jesus, a good motto to adopt could well
be this dynamic motto—"Always Ready."

An African ricksha man in Johannesburg, South
Africa, expressed his faith in a soon-coming Saviour
by placing coverings over the wheels of his ricksha
with these words printed on them: "Jesus is coming
again soon! Are you ready to meet Him?"

Every person must face this question, and face
it honestly: Am I really ready to meet Jesus when
He comes?

Describing that day of judgment, when all cases

are finally decided, Jesus says, "Then shall two be in the field; the one shall be taken, and the other left. Two women shall be grinding at the mill; the one shall be taken, and the other left." Matthew 24: 40, 41.

"Therefore be ye also ready: for in such an hour as ye think not the Son of man cometh." Verse 44.

How may we be ready? First, we must surrender and make confession of our sins. There must be victory over evil in our lives. We must study God's Word and by His help bring our lives into conformity with all revealed truth. The Golden Rule will govern our relationship with others. Then we will be truly ready to meet Jesus with joy and gladness.

"Oh that my words were now written!
Oh that they were printed in a book!
That they were graven with an iron pen
and lead in the rock for ever!
For I know that my redeemer liveth,
and that he shall stand
at the latter day upon the earth:
And though after my skin
worms destroy this body,
Yet in my flesh shall I see God:
Whom I shall see for myself,
and mine eyes shall behold,
and not another."

Job 19:23-27.

# SECTION VI

# Strange Ideas About Death

Years ago in India a Jain monk came to visit me in a travelers' bungalow. Over the lower part of his face he wore a thin cotton mask; and as he walked up the roadway, he used a small broom to brush the pathway ahead of him. The Jains, a branch of the Hindu religion, believe in transmigration of the soul. They think that when a person dies he assumes some other form of existence, so that in his next reincarnation a man may live again as a cow, a monkey, or an insect. The Jain wore a mask and swept the path in order to avoid swallowing a gnat or stepping on a beetle and thereby killing some friend or relative who may have become an insect.

"Man dieth, and wasteth away: yea, man giveth up the ghost, and where is he?" Job asked. (Job 14: 10.) This is a good question, one of interest and concern to every man. We all have lost a loved one. We all face death ourselves someday, and we need to have our questions about death answered.

What is death? How long does it last? There are many voices in the world purporting to answer these questions.

While I was in India, I lived for some years near a Zoroastrian Tower of Silence, where the followers

140

The devout Hindu, in his regard for life, wears a
mask lest he breathe in and destroy a gnat.

of Zoroaster place the bodies of their dead on grates.
Vultures denude the bones in seconds, thus carrying,
they believe, the soul of the departed to his reward.

The Buddhist believes in an ultimate state called
Nirvana. He looks forward to a condition of blissful
oblivion where care, pain, love, or other external
reality will not exist.

Orthodox Mr. Average Christian believes that
good people go to heaven and bad people go to hell
when they die.

What *does* happen to a person when he dies?
Where does he go?

*Tuesday*

# What Happens After Death?

The best way to learn something about a place
you have never visited is to talk with someone who
has been there. On one occasion while I was traveling by plane, a man in the seat ahead of me
expounded at great length about Africa to his seat-
mate. I listened intently, for I was interested in
Africa. I had lived there for six years and traveled
in many of its countries; though I laid no claim to
being an expert on the subject, I knew a little about
the situation there. As I listened, questions surged
through my mind. What the man was saying simply

did not square with the facts as I knew them, and I was not surprised when he climaxed his assessment of Africa and her problems with a frank, "Well, that's what I think about the situation in Africa today and what should be done." He paused, then continued, "Of course, I've never been there, but that's my opinion."

It is, of course, far better to ask someone who has been there when you wish to learn about a place you have never visited.

You and I have never tasted death, never gone down into the tomb, never come back with the answer to, What happens to a person when he dies? Where does he go? What lies beyond the tomb? But I know Someone who has!

Jesus Christ, God's only Son, knows what is in the tomb, for He has been there. He knows what happens when man dies, for He died. He came back to answer our question: "I am he that liveth, and was dead; and, behold, I am alive for evermore, . . . and have the keys of hell and of death." Revelation 1:18. He is the ultimate authority on death. Instead of having to deal with unproven theories, He speaks from experience. He has conquered death and knows its secrets.

Jesus knows, and He has the answer to life's most profound question. We, too, may know the answer to this question.

*Wednesday*

# How Jesus Explained Death

We will never go wrong following Jesus' example or accepting His teachings. He tells us about death in this interesting experience of His ministry:

"Now there was a man by the name of Lazarus who became seriously ill. He lived in Bethany, the village where Mary and her sister Martha lived. . . . So the sisters sent word to Jesus: 'Lord, your friend is very ill.' " John 11:1-3, Phillips.

We might wonder why Jesus did not immediately return to Bethany to help Lazarus. But John states, "When he heard of Lazarus' illness he stayed where he was two days longer." Verse 6. Then, as the little group made their way slowly back to Judea, they spoke of Lazarus and his illness.

Jesus said, " 'Our friend Lazarus has fallen asleep, but I am going to wake him up.' At this, his disciples said, 'Lord, if he has fallen asleep, he will be all right.' Actually Jesus had spoken about his death, but they thought that he was speaking about falling into natural sleep. This made Jesus tell them quite plainly: 'Lazarus has died.' " Verses 11-14.

The King James Version gives the same doctrine in a little less storylike form. Whichever version you prefer, Jesus spoke of death as being a sleep: "Our friend Lazarus sleepeth." Then He says plainly, "Lazarus is dead."

What a beautiful thought: Death is an unconscious sleep. For the one who believes in Jesus it removes all that is dreadful in death. It is rest after a busy life. There is no knowledge of passing time. He awakes on the resurrection morning welcomed by a coming Life-giver.

*Thursday*

# A Man Restored From Death

The Saviour's meeting with Mary and Martha was a sad, tearful one for the two women. Lazarus, their brother, had died and for four days had been in his tomb.

" 'If only you had been here, Lord,' said Martha, 'my brother would never have died.' "

" 'Your brother will rise again,' Jesus replied to her.

" 'I know,' said Martha, 'that he will rise again in the resurrection at the last day.'

" 'I myself am the resurrection and the life,' Jesus told her."

"When Jesus saw Mary weep and noticed the tears of the Jews who came with her, he was deeply moved and visibly distressed."

" 'Where have you put him?' he asked.

" 'Lord, come and see,' they replied, and at this Jesus himself wept."

"Jesus . . . went on to the grave. It was a cave, and a stone lay in front of it.

" 'Take away the stone,' said Jesus.

" 'But, Lord,' said Martha, . . . 'he has been dead four days. By this time he will be decaying. . . .'

"Then they took the stone away."

After prayer Jesus "called out in a loud voice, 'Lazarus, come out!' " (John 11:21, 23-25, 33-35, 38, 41, 43, Phillips.)

Martha knew that when a loved one dies, he sleeps in the tomb until the resurrection morning. Only Jesus, who symbolizes resurrection and life, could change that. The Saviour did not say to his dead friend, "Lazarus, come down from heaven." Nor did He say, "Lazarus, come up from hell or from purgatory." He knew Lazarus was not in any of these places, and He said simply, "Lazarus, come forth from the tomb."

This wonderful answer to our question as to the whereabouts of the dead should comfort each person who has lost a loved one, and who must himself meet this experience. Like a person falling asleep after a long, arduous day, when a person dies he falls into the deepest possible of sleeps. A loving God watches over His own and marks their resting-places.

*Friday*

# Death Is a Sleep

When Jesus taught that death is a sleep, He confirmed what writers of the Old Testament had expounded centuries earlier. His stamp of approval was placed on similar tenets recorded by the apostles who produced the New Testament.

Job spoke of death as an unconscious sleep. He said, "So man lieth down, and riseth not: till the heavens be no more, they shall not awake, nor be raised out of their sleep." Job 14:12.

The psalmist David also wrote about "the sleep of death." (Psalm 13:3.) Centuries later Luke in his Book of Acts referred to David and what had happened to him after death. David was a man after God's own heart, according to the Scriptures. Surely if any saint could go immediately to the gloryland, David would have gone. Luke quotes some of what Peter said while he was under the influence of the Holy Spirit at Pentecost centuries after David's death: "David is not ascended into the heavens." Acts 2:34. Later Luke quoted part of what Paul said at Antioch: "For David, after he had served his own generation by the will of God, fell on sleep, and was laid unto his fathers, and saw corruption." Acts 13:36. David not only taught that death was a sleep, he experienced that sleep himself, according to the Scriptures.

The prophet Daniel, looking forward to a resurrection of the righteous and of the wicked, prophesied, "Many of them that *sleep* in the dust of the earth shall *awake,* some to everlasting life, and some to shame and everlasting contempt." Daniel 12:2.

Referring to saints who had seen Christ after His resurrection but who had since died, Paul says, "Some are fallen asleep." 1 Corinthians 15:6. Writing of the saints of all ages awaiting the resurrection morning, the apostle describes them as those who "are asleep." (1 Thessalonians 4:13.) After Stephen was stoned to death by a mob, Luke wrote that "he fell asleep." (Acts 7:60.)

Thus Jesus and the inspired Bible writers agree that death is a sleep.

*Saturday*

# Is There an Immortal Soul?

While riding through the Southwest listening to my car radio, I heard a preacher describing a book he had recently written on the "immortal soul." "It is filled with choice Bible texts on the subject," he said. Are there enough texts on the immortal soul to fill a book? I wondered.

This phrase, "immortal soul," is used freely in Christian circles. But when I open my Bible, I learn that there is but one place in all Scripture where the word *immortal* appears. This is in the Book of First Timothy, but the reference is not to man's soul, man's spirit, man's body, or even to man at all. The passage states, "Now unto the King eternal, *immortal*, invisible, the only wise God." 1 Timothy 1: 17. Thus the reference is actually to God, who alone possesses inherent immortality, and not to man. (1 Timothy 6:16.)

Man, by nature, is mortal. (Job 4:17.) *Mortal*, as defined in a dictionary, means "subject to death." Unless we live to see Jesus come, every one of us someday will die. We are mortal—subject to death. The words *soul* and *spirit* appear about nine hundred times in Scripture. But never once is the word *immortal* used to describe either. Biblical writers missed over nine hundred opportunities of stating that the soul is immortal, if indeed it were.

But, thank God, immortality may be ours. It is a gift of God "brought . . . to light through the gospel." (2 Timothy 1:10.) It is bestowed not at death but, as Paul says, at the time of the first resurrection: "At the last trump . . . we shall be changed. . . . This mortal must put on immortality." 1 Corinthians 15:52, 53.

Immortality may be ours, not by birth or by

nature, but as a precious gift from the hand of God
bestowed *at the time of Christ's appearing!*

*Sunday*

# Death Is Not Life

"Put not your trust in princes, nor in the son of
man, in whom there is no help. His breath goeth
forth, he returneth to his earth; in that very day his
thoughts perish" (Psalm 146:3, 4), wrote the
psalmist, describing what takes place when a person dies.

"Death is not a modification of life. Death is not
a continuation of life in changed conditions. Death
is not a release into a fuller life. Death is not life
in misery. Death is not life in happiness. Death is
not life at all, in any condition whether good or bad.
To die is not to live. To die is to stop living. Death
is a complete cessation of life.

"Death does not mean to go to heaven. Death
does not mean to go to hell. Death does not mean
to go to purgatory. Death does not mean to go any-
where. Death means an end of life."—C. B. Haynes,
*The Other Side of Death,* p. 37.

Further light is given on the subject by the Scriptures: "For the living know that they shall die: but
the dead know not any thing, neither have they any

more a reward; for the memory of them is forgotten. Also their love, and their hatred, and their envy, is now perished." Ecclesiastes 9:5, 6.

There is no intelligence or knowledge in death. If a saint were in heaven, certainly he would possess both. But the mortal state of man is emphasized by this passage: "His sons come to honour, and he knoweth it not; and they are brought low, but he perceiveth it not of them." Job 14:21.

*Monday*

# Death Need Not Be Final

A gay little golden-haired girl was playing ball with a playmate by the side of a busy street. She missed one catch, and the ball rolled onto the busy thoroughfare, and she dashed after it. There was a screeching of brakes as an oncoming motorist sought to avoid hitting the child, but his efforts failed. Moments later spectators picked up the broken little body and bore it tenderly to a distraught mother.

A few days later words of comfort were spoken by the pastor at the church nearby. After all the others had left the church, father and mother stood by the casket for one last look at their tiny darling.

The father, a strapping fellow, had no faith to cling to in such an hour. For him death was the end.

As he looked down upon the still white form before him, he ran his fingers through the child's golden tresses one last time. "Good-bye, my little girl—forever," the anguished words came, as his big frame shook with sobs.

The heart of the mother was bleeding, too. To lose her precious daughter so suddenly shook her deeply, but she had a faith—confidence in a coming Life-giver—that buoyed her up in this trying hour. For her there was a returning Saviour, a resurrection morning. Her voice was filled with hope as she said, "Good-bye, my little one. Mother will *see you in the morning!*"

For the child of faith the grave is not the end. "I am the resurrection, and the life: he that believeth in me, though he were dead, yet shall he live," Jesus once said to sorrowing friends. (John 11:25.)

This precious assurance is for every child of God today.

*Tuesday*

# In Mercy, God Leads

It is difficult to see beyond our tears. When the best in life has suddenly been taken from us, it is not always easy to understand how "to those who love God, . . . everything that happens fits into a pattern for good." (Romans 8:28, Phillips.)

But that is God's promise to us. With an eternity ahead, our short lives here will seem very different. Then we will understand why heartaches and trials had to be a part of us. From that vantage point we may understand God's leading and realize that we could not have chosen any better way.

God promises through the psalmist, "They that sow in tears shall reap in joy." Psalm 126:5.

When death takes a loved one, remember that "precious in the sight of the Lord is the death of his saints." (Psalm 116:15.) This seems an unusual statement for the psalmist to make. Why does he say it this way? The answer is that when a child of God is taken from this valley of tears, he is beyond the reach of the evil one. Sleeping, he awaits the resurrection morning. Satan can no longer tempt him or bring to him trials and difficulties. He belongs to Jesus. The death of such a person is indeed "precious in the sight of the Lord."

John makes a similar statement: "Blessed are the dead which die in the Lord from henceforth: Yea, saith the Spirit, that they may rest from their labours; and their works do follow them." Revelation 14:13.

The next scene John saw was that of Jesus coming in the clouds of heaven: "And I looked, and behold a white cloud, and upon the cloud one sat like unto the Son of man, having on his head a golden crown, and in his hand a sharp sickle." Verse 14.

Just before Jesus returns, there will be great difficulties and misery in the world. Daniel called this period "a time of trouble, such as never was since there was a nation." (Daniel 12:1.) The Lord in His mercy will spare some of His people these difficult experiences by permitting them to fall asleep in Jesus "that they may rest from their labours," John says.

Paul comforts us with the admonition, "Sorrow not, even as others which have no hope." 1 Thessalonians 4:13.

> "There's no disappointment in heaven,
>     No weariness, sorrow or pain;
> No hearts that are bleeding and broken,
>     No song with a minor refrain;
> The clouds of our earthly horizon
>     Will never appear in the sky,
> For all will be sunshine and gladness,
>     With never a sob nor a sigh."
>
> —*F. M. Lehman.*

*Wednesday*

# Yes, Jesus Cares

Many years ago I sat in a small church in Florida listening to this hymn sung by a quartet:

> "Does Jesus care when I've said 'good-bye'
>     To the dearest on earth to me,
>     And my sad heart aches
>     Till it nearly breaks—
>     Is this aught to Him? does He see?"

The words echoed a question tugging painfully at my heart, for the occasion was my mother's funeral. Did Jesus really care when I said good-bye to the dearest on earth to me?

Then with beautiful assurance the words of the chorus rang out:

> "O yes, He cares, I know He cares,
>     His heart is touched with my grief;
>     When the days are weary,
>     The long nights dreary,
>     I know my Saviour cares."
>
> *—Frank E. Graeff.*

Friend of mine, when our sad hearts ache till they nearly break, what a comfort it is to know that

Jesus *does* care, that His great heart of love is touched with our grief.

When we walk with loved ones into the valley of the shadow of death, there is little lasting comfort that human lips can speak. Our friends take us by the hand and speak a few words, and we deeply appreciate their sympathy, but words do not fully heal a breaking heart. Only the certainty of God's words —His promises—can truly soothe the aching heart.

Jesus was "a man of sorrows, and acquainted with grief. . . . He hath borne our griefs, and carried our sorrows." (Isaiah 53:3, 4.) On Calvary the mental agony was greater than the physical torture, and Jesus died of a broken heart. He does indeed understand our anguish, for He, too, has suffered.

He has shown through the ages how much He cares. "For he said, Surely they are my people: . . . he was their Saviour. In all their affliction he was afflicted, and the angel of his presence saved them: in his love and in his pity he redeemed them; and he bare them, and carried them all the days of old." Isaiah 63:8, 9.

It is true, as Paul says, that "we have not an high priest which cannot be touched with the feeling of our infirmities." (Hebrews 4:15.) As the Man of sorrows, acquainted with grief, Christ enters into our heartaches and disappointments.

These words were written by one who knew

from personal experience that Jesus cares: "Our heavenly Father is never unmindful of those whom sorrow has touched. . . . To every stricken one, Jesus comes with the ministry of healing. The life of bereavement, pain, and suffering may be brightened by precious revealings of His presence."—Ellen G. White, *Thoughts From the Mount of Blessing,* pp. 11, 12.

Today, if your heart is aching because you have lost a loved one, look up, behold your loving Father in heaven with His message of comfort for you. Wise Augustine said, "Let God cover thy wounds: do not thou." Then he explains that when you try to cover your wounds alone, the hurt is only concealed, but that if God does it for you they are healed.

# SECTION VII

# A Mirror Tells the Truth

It happened many years ago on a beautiful South Pacific island. The queen had never seen herself in a mirror, so she did not know how truly ugly she was. One day a ship brought a large consignment of mirrors to the island, and the natives bought them eagerly. The queen, noticing the brisk trading in mirrors, bought one.

Then the sad truth was revealed to her—she was indeed ugly. No woman enjoys being ugly, but a queen can do something about it, and this queen did. She was so indignant over the truth the mirror revealed that she decided all mirrors should be confiscated and destroyed.

James describes the law of God as a mirror. "For if any be a hearer of the word, and not a doer, he is like unto a man beholding his natural face in a glass: for he beholdeth himself, and goeth his way, and straightway forgetteth what manner of man he was. But whoso looketh unto the perfect law of liberty, and continueth therein, he being not a forgetful hearer, but a doer of the work, this man shall be blessed in his deed." James 1:23-25.

The law, like a mirror, tells us if our spiritual face is dirty or our lives are sin-stained.

The ugly queen could destroy all mirrors—man cannot escape his reflection in God's law.

If the spiritual mirror tells you that your face is soiled and needs washing, what will you do to remedy the situation? Try to wash your face with the mirror? Give it away because it reveals a sad fact disagreeable to you? Neither course of action would make your face clean.

*Friday*

# What Do You Look Like to God?

We must discover the true relationship existing between the law of God and the gospel. There are those in the world today who believe and teach that by strictly keeping the law of God one may somehow, someday, assume the moral finery of a Saul of Tarsus and be saved. Paul himself gainsays such a possibility when he says, "By the deeds of the law there shall no flesh be justified in his sight." Romans 3:20. No one is going to work his way into heaven merely because he outwardly keeps the commandments of God.

Still others contend that the claims of God's law must be forever banished if one is to enjoy the full freedom of the gospel. "Away with the old yoke of bondage," they shout, despite the fact that God says His "law is holy, . . . and just, and good." (Romans 7:12.)

6

Such a course plunges us into the ditch on the other side of the road. It would be much the same for me to assert that I was going to become a good citizen of my city by doing away with all the laws and ordinances enacted to ensure the peace and prosperity of my community. Although a person can never hope to save himself through outward conformity to the commandments of God, the law does have its place in the gospel message, just as the law of my city has its place in the maintenance of peace and order.

The part the law of God plays in man's redemption is singular and vital—it reveals sin to the individual and impresses upon the sinner his need of a Saviour. The law does not save us; it merely points out sin in our lives. Only Jesus Christ, the Lamb of God, can save us. The law is God's sin detector, for "by the law is the knowledge of sin." (Romans 3: 20.) "Indeed it is the straightedge of the Law that shows us how crooked we are," Phillips puts it in his translation of Paul's words.

The apostle declared that a glimpse of the commandments revealed to him his own sin: "I had not known sin, but by the law: for I had not known lust, except the law had said, Thou shalt not covet." Romans 7:7.

Have you had a look at the Ten Commandments recently to see how you appear in God's sight?

*Saturday*

# The Rock Breaker

Among the rocky ruins of the ancient Roman city of Gerasa, built centuries ago when the legions of the Caesars occupied the eastern frontier of what is now Syria, is to be found in abundance a plant known as saxifrage. The saxifrage plant derives its name from two Latin words (*saxi* and *frangere*) which mean literally "to break rock."

Gerasa once was a flourishing, prosperous city, receiving most of its revenue from the sale of incense used by pagans in various forms of worship. As the gospel penetrated this section of the Roman empire and the worship of God displaced idol worship, the importance of Gerasa waned. Trade declined; gradually the city fell into decay.

Now, centuries later, through the rocky ruins of ancient Gerasa, the saxifrage plant, the "rock breaker," still flourishes as it pushes asunder the crumbling colonnades of primitive paganism.

Such also is the power of the gospel. It is indeed a rock breaker. Hearts, apparently as unyielding as flint, have been broken by the simple story of a Saviour's love of and death for sinners.

The word *gospel* in the original language of the New Testament is the Greek word *euaggelion,* meaning literally "good news." Truly, the story of God's Son, given to a world which the prophet Isaiah describes as being covered by "gross darkness" (Isaiah 60:2), is indeed good news.

Paul declares that the gospel is far more than a mere story, much more than good news. He wrote, "I am not ashamed of the gospel of Christ: for it is the power of God unto salvation to every one that believeth." Romans 1:16.

"Our Saviour Jesus Christ," Paul says, "hath abolished death, and hath brought life and immortality to light through the gospel." 2 Timothy 1:10. "The wages of sin is death," he writes further; "but the gift of God is eternal life through Jesus Christ our Lord." Romans 6:23. Sin says, "Die!" But through Christ we may live.

In the tropical forests of the West Indies grows the manchineel tree, bearing an apple-shaped fruit. The milky juice of this tree is very poisonous. Among these deadly trees grows a species of fig tree whose sap, if applied in time, it is claimed, will counteract the effects of the manchineel poisoning.

Such is the power of the gospel if applied in faith to the sin-sick soul. The blood of Christ can make the vilest sinner whole. "Thou shalt call his name Jesus," the angel instructed Mary, "for he shall save his people from their sins." Matthew 1:21.

The gospel is the power of God to save men and

women. From what do we need to be saved? The text in Matthew's Gospel contains the answer, "He shall save his people from their sins."

*Sunday*

# What Is Sin?

What is sin? Some say that sin is drinking, swearing, gambling, stealing, or evil thinking. These various ideas indicate different evaluations of what is right and what is wrong, according to the individual. One person insists that drinking is wrong; another feels there is no harm in "moderate" indulgence. One writer declared that he was sure God was not annoyed by cursing, that He looked upon it as a natural manner of letting off steam occasionally. To another, however, using the name of God as part of a curse phrase is highly offensive.

The ancient Greeks referred to their mistakes by a word which means "bad shots." To them, their sins were something bound to occur. There was nothing they could do about them, so it was best to forget their mistakes. Such was the pagan attitude toward sin.

When we turn to the writings of John the beloved, we discover an all-inclusive definition of sin. He sums up all categories of evil in these words:

"Whosoever committeth sin transgresseth also the law: for sin is the transgression of the law." 1 John 3:4.

Thus the violation of any one of the Ten Commandments constitutes sin. If I take the name of the Lord in vain, in contradiction of the third precept, I sin. If I steal, I sin, for the commandment says, "Thou shalt not steal." In flouting its warning, I transgress the law of God. If I erect strange gods in my heart, I sin. Each is mentioned in the Ten Commandments as contrary to the will and character of God.

Sin, as defined in the Bible, is breaking the law of God.

*Monday*

# The Gospel–A Way of Escape

There·are those who speak of the dispensation of the law and the dispensation of the gospel as though the two were entirely separate, perhaps even antagonistic one to the other. Some clerics declare that the gospel supersedes the law and completely abrogates its claims upon man. But how can this be?

The gospel tells about God's plan to save man. Save him from what? Why, to save him from sin! What is sin? God says it is the violation of any of the Ten Commandments. (1 John 3:4.) When we break the commandments, we earn death, for "the wages of sin is death." The gospel, however, brings the good news that God has provided a way of escape. Jesus died in our place that we may with impunity accept His substitutionary death.

This, then, brings us to another question, and it is a very vital one: Does the preaching of the gospel countermand, or displace, the precepts of the Decalogue? We have already noted that the only reason for the existence of the gospel is to save men from sin, "the transgression of the law." Paul says plainly, "Where no law is, there is no transgression." Romans 4:15.

If the law was abolished with the advent of the gospel, then, the apostle declares, there would no longer be any transgression—no sin in the world. Paul emphasizes this further by stating, "Sin is not imputed when there is no law." Romans 5:13.

So if there is no law, there is no sin. If there is no sin, there is no need of the gospel. Rather than one's being antagonistic toward the other and existing apart in different dispensations, the law and the gospel in reality are inseparable. Because the commandments have been broken and the sinner deserves to die, we have the gospel to bring hope to the lost. The gospel would not be needed if there were no sin. The very fact of sin's presence on every hand today loudly proclaims mankind's need of the gospel.

All about us we see the aftermath of sin's de-
structive power. God's law is still being broken.
There are today murderers, thieves, evil-speaking
and evil-thinking men and women, greedy and
grasping people, godless individuals, who need
salvation through the gospel.

Thank God, the gospel provides a way of escape
for the repentant sinner who has broken God's
holy law.

*Tuesday*

# Real Meaning of the Law

Centuries before Jesus was born in Bethlehem,
the Old Testament prophet Isaiah foretold what the
Saviour's attitude toward the Ten Commandments
would be, in these words: "He will magnify the law,
and make it honourable." Isaiah 42:21.

*Magnify* means "to extol, to laud, to cause to be
held in greater esteem and respect; to increase in
significance, to enlarge in fact."

According to Isaiah, then, Jesus would extol
the law, would cause the commandments to be held
in greater esteem, to increase in significance. I've
heard it said that Jesus came to do away with the
Ten Commandments, but Isaiah certainly doesn't

indicate that Christ came to this world to repeal the divine set of laws God had given centuries before.

How did Jesus "magnify" the law? How did He make it more significant? The letter of the law warns, "Thou shalt not kill." Exodus 20:13. Jesus magnified this commandment by explaining that more than murder was forbidden: "I say unto you, That whosoever is angry with his brother without a cause shall be in danger of the judgment." Matthew 5:22. Hatred is the father of murder. Job says that "wrath killeth." (Job 5:2.) Jesus made the sixth commandment more significant, more meaningful, by declaring that it forbids hatred as well as the overt act of murder.

The letter of the law warns against adultery. Jesus magnified or enlarged the seventh commandment by including lustful contemplation—evil thinking. "I say unto you, That whosoever looketh on a woman to lust after her, hath committed adultery with her already in his heart." Matthew 5:28. In both cases Christ went beyond the surface of the laws to the great principles behind them.

Jesus did not come to do away with the law of God. He came to magnify that law, to make it more significant in the everyday activities of men that it might be held in greater esteem. He did not come to abolish the law of God—not by the farthest stretch of the imagination.

*Wednesday*

# Christ Came to Set an Example

"You must not think that I have come to abolish the Law or the Prophets; I have not come to abolish them but to complete them. Indeed, I assure you that, while Heaven and earth last, the Law will not lose a single dot or comma until its purpose is complete." In these words Phillips translates Matthew 5:17, 18. The King James Version says the same thing, but Phillips puts the Saviour's words in more modern, up-to-the-minute speech.

"I am not come to destroy, but to fulfil." Some suggest that the word *fulfill* used here means "to do away with." This, of course, is not consistent with Bible usage as we may well note from the words of Christ at the time of His baptism: "And Jesus answering said unto him [John the Baptist], Suffer it to be so now: for thus it becometh us to *fulfil all righteousness*. Then he suffered him." Matthew 3:15.

Jesus here states that His baptism is part of His plan to *fulfill* all righteousness. If a person is to be consistent in his contention that to fulfill means "to do away with" when it appears in connection with the law in Matthew 5:17, 18, then the position must also be taken that Christ meant that He was going "to do away with" all righteousness at His baptism.

For this position, of course, no one would contend.
Actually the word *fulfill,* as used in Matthew, carries
the meaning of "fully preaching" and it is so translated from the original Greek in Colossians 1:25.
(See The Berkeley Version.) Rather than do away
with the commandments, Jesus came to preach and
to live out their eternal precepts fully in His earthly
ministry, so that men could better understand how
to live by the law as a result of His example.

*Thursday*

# Are You Truly Free?

"None of the old law for me," the man declared
indignantly. "I am free from the old bondage. I
want you to know that the blood of Christ makes
me *free!*"

I was a bit taken aback by the outburst, but because I had heard such theology propounded before,
I was not too surprised when my new acquaintance
erupted with such vehemence. We had been discuss-
ing the Christian's relationship to the law of God.

"When Jesus Christ died upon the cross of Calvary, He did away with the commandments, and I
am *free,* I tell you—*free!*" he continued vigorously.

"It is certainly true," I ventured patiently. " 'If

the Son therefore shall make you free, ye shall be free indeed,' " I said, quoting John 8:36.

My friend began to smile. I had seen the light, he was sure.

But I was not through explaining. I said to him, "Paul explains what the blood of Christ frees us from. In the sixth chapter of Romans—twice in verses 18 and 22—the apostle says we are freed from *sin*—not freed from the law." Then we continued to study the Bible together.

The person who *breaks* the law is not one who long enjoys freedom. In fact, the lawbreaker is the one who loses his freedom. The jails are full of men and women who have lost their liberty when they broke the law. Normally, those who *keep* the law are the ones who enjoy freedom. They are not the ones who are a danger to society. It is only those who either break the law or who try to get around it. It is the same in spiritual society.

"I will walk at liberty," the psalmist asserted, "for I seek thy precepts." Psalm 119:45. The person whose life is in harmony with the commandments of God, one who, as Peter says, is "not using . . . liberty for a cloke" (1 Peter 2:16), is truly free in Christ Jesus. In fact, James speaks of the Ten Commandments as the "perfect law of liberty." (James 1:25.)

Only in true obedience can we find true freedom.

*Friday*

# "But for the Grace of God . . ."

One morning a well-known British preacher was strolling along a London street with a friend. In the gutter of the street along which they were walking lay a poor shell of humanity. His hair and beard were matted, giving evidence that he had long been a stranger to soap and water. His eyes were bleary and bloodshot, his nose bulbous and red. The rags partially covering his weakened frame could scarcely be called a suit of clothes, they were so filthy and full of holes. Beside him lay an empty bottle, mute testimony of the tragedy that had overtaken the hapless wretch. Unsteadily the old derelict pulled himself to his feet and shuffled down the street.

As the man of God and his friend witnessed the pitiful sight, the minister turned to his companion and, with a hint of emotion in his voice, said, "George, there but for the grace of God go I!"

Yes, my friend, there, figuratively speaking, but for the grace of God, goes a whole world of judgment-bound sinners! Did you ever stop to think just what the world would be like had not the grace of God interposed between the sinner and the inevitable result of transgression? It makes me shudder to contemplate such a scene.

In religious circles today we hear a great deal about grace. We speak of being "saved by grace." We say that God's grace is sufficient for us. We speak of a dispensation of grace and of being "under grace." Although we make frequent reference to this wonderfully meaningful word, do we fully understand what grace truly is?

*Saturday*

# The Function of Grace

Some people may read Romans 6:14 and prematurely conclude that the law and grace are antagonistic. In this passage the apostle says, "For sin shall not have dominion over you: for ye are not under the law, but under grace."

To understand fully the meaning of this passage of Scripture, one must be familiar with its context. The early verses of the chapter describe the experience of an individual who has been born again, one whose life is now in harmony with all the commandments. Such a person is not under the curse or penalty of the law, but, as a sinner deserving to die, he has received unmerited favor from Heaven, and is, therefore, "under grace." The penalty of the broken law no longer hangs over him.

Does grace then abolish the law? Paul hastens

to assure us that he would not wish to convey such an impression. "What then? shall we sin [transgress the law], because we are not under the law, but under grace? God forbid." Verse 15.

Remember that grace is pardon or unmerited favor extended when law has been violated. If there is no law, there will be no violations, and consequently no need for grace. Grace is not something that exists apart from law; but, because a law exists and has been broken, grace is necessary to save the lawbreaker. Paul makes this clear in Romans 4:15: "Where no law is, there is no transgression."

Is there sin in the world today? All will agree that sin reigns on every hand. Then there must be law, for Paul makes clear that there is no sin if there is no law. No law, no transgression; no transgression, no need of grace.

Suppose you are arrested for writing a letter to your wife and hailed into court on such a charge. What would be your reaction if the judge should say, "Well, there is no law against writing a letter to your wife, so I will pardon you"? Rightfully you would be indignant. Since no law existed forbidding such correspondence, you would not be guilty of any misdemeanor and would need no pardon or grace. No law, no transgression. No transgression, no need of grace! When a man strays from "the straight and narrow road" and runs afoul of the law, deserving punishment, only *then* does he need pardon or grace.

Law and grace are inseparable. They have been thus all through the ages. No law, no transgression; no transgression, no need of grace.

*Sunday*

# The Meaning of Grace

Very early on a rainy morning, before the sun was up, I was entering the suburbs of a Southern city. The traffic light was amber as I was about to enter the intersection, so I drove right on through. Evidently the amber became red before I had cleared the intersection, for very shortly my wife nudged me. "A patrol car is behind signaling you to stop," she said.

Never being a person to argue with the law, I quickly pulled to one side and stopped. Before the officer could get out I was by his car. "What is it, Officer?" I asked, with a show of great calm.

"Didn't you drive through a red light back there?" he asked.

"Yes, Officer, I did," I confessed. "It was raining, and I was fearful of applying my brakes too quickly. I was afraid I might skid."

"You wouldn't have needed to worry about that

if you hadn't been driving sixty miles an hour," he said dryly.

"Was I going sixty miles an hour?" I asked incredulously.

"You sure were," he replied.

"Then I was wrong, Officer, wasn't I?" Truth was my only hope of mercy.

By this time the officer had scrutinized my driver's license and noted that I was a minister; and perhaps influenced by the fact that traffic was very light at that early hour and also by my honest admission of guilt, he continued, "Well, Preacher, take it easy through here next time. This is a forty-five-mile-an-hour zone."

I thanked him, breathed a sigh of relief, and drove on. I had broken the law. I deserved punishment. A kind patrolman had "let me off." It was treatment I did not deserve. Theologically, I was "under grace," for I had been the recipient of a pardon I did not merit.

Grace, the Apostle Paul defines, is "God's unmerited favor," "unearned and undeserved favor." (Romans 5:20, 21, The Amplified New Testament.)

You and I are sinners. We have broken God's law. We deserve to die. Jesus' blood provides a pardon we do not deserve. This is God's grace.

God has myriads of angels who, out of love, serve and obey Him. He loves them, but He does not give them grace. They have never sinned and therefore do not need it—nor have they ever needed it. Only to undeserving human beings is grace given. It is a gift sent to us; we did not ask for it. One of the mysteries of God is that He gives grace to all who want it, not because we deserve it, but because we need it. It is our need that qualifies us to receive this wonderful gift.

*Monday*

# Relationship Between Grace and Law

After the happy ending to my experience with the traffic patrolman, do you think I drove through all the traffic lights that were against me that morning? Do you suppose I reasoned, "Well, I have been pardoned, I am under grace now; I don't need to worry about the law anymore"? Did the fact that I was under grace free me from the laws of the city afterward?

I can assure you that no such reasoning muddled my thinking that day. Because the officer had so kindly pardoned me, because I was "under grace" as it were, I drove more carefully than before. I observed the traffic laws more strictly than ever. I was thankful I had escaped punishment through the kindness of a patrolman to an out-of-town driver.

Now how does this work in the Christian's journey to the kingdom? When he is "under grace," does this provide license to disregard the claims of the law? Let us note what Paul has to say about it:

"Now what is our response to be?" the apostle asks. "Shall we sin to our heart's content and see how far we can exploit the grace of God? What a ghastly thought! We, who have died to sin—how could we live in sin a moment longer?" Romans 6:1, 2, Phillips.

"Sin is the transgression of the law." 1 John 3:4. Grace is the unmerited favor God extends to the repentant sinner. In the light of these Scriptural truths we could read Paul's words, without doing them violence, thus: "Shall we continue to break the law that grace may abound? God forbid!" Inspiration makes it plain that grace does not provide license to disregard the Ten Commandments. Rather, it makes us under more obligation than ever before to keep our lives in harmony with His law because of His grace and goodness.

# SECTION VIII

# Embarrassment and Enlightenment

It was one of those moments of truth that gives birth to both embarrassment and enlightenment.

In a large city the mayor was trying to rally support for a Sunday-closing bill. Anxious to enlist the help of the churches, he called a meeting especially slanted toward churchgoing people. As a backdrop behind the speakers' platform he hung a huge calendar, with all the Sundays painted red, and a large chart of the Ten Commandments.

The meeting was barely under way when a man rose and addressed the chairman. "Your Honor," he began, "which day of the week *is* the Sabbath?"

"The seventh, of course," the mayor replied, pointing to the fourth commandment behind him. "Read it yourself!"

"Sir, that is what I have been doing," the man continued, "and I am greatly confused. Your calendar, the fourth commandment, and your proposal do not agree. The fourth commandment says the *seventh* day is the Sabbath; your calendar clearly reveals that *Saturday,* not Sunday, is the seventh day of the week. Now you want us to vote a Sunday-closing law because keeping stores open on Sunday is a violation of the fourth commandment. Your

181

Honor, I believe something is wrong someplace."

Turning, the mayor looked first at the calendar, then at the Ten Commandments in stunned disbelief. Embarrassed, the honest mayor admitted his mistake, and the Sunday-closing bill soon lost momentum.

Houston's mayor is not the first person to become perplexed when he looks at the fourth commandment and then at the calendar. Thousands have sincerely wondered why most Christians observe Sunday, the first day of the week, when the fourth commandment clearly states, "The seventh day is the sabbath of the Lord thy God." Exodus 20:10. This is something worth looking into.

*Wednesday*

# Why God Made the Sabbath

"The sabbath was made for man," Christ said. (Mark 2:27.) God made the seventh-day Sabbath to be a day of rest. After six days of toil the human body needs relaxation. To help meet the physical needs of man God set aside *His* rest day (Genesis 2:3) to be *man's* rest day as well. "In it thou shalt not do any work" (Exodus 20:10), He commanded. All the secular activities of the busy week are to be laid aside and this holy day especially dedicated to an intimate relationship between God and man so that this day of rest becomes "a delight, the holy of the Lord, honourable." (Isaiah 58:13.)

The seventh-day Sabbath was given as a memorial to God's creative power. "Remember the sabbath day, to keep it holy." "For in six days the Lord made heaven and earth, the sea, and all that in them is." Exodus 20:8, 11. If, through the centuries, man had faithfully remembered the Creator on the day He set aside as a memorial to creation, there would today be no evolutionists, no doubters of the fundamental teachings of God's Word. When man failed to "remember the sabbath," he soon forgot the Lord of the Sabbath—the Creator—thus opening the floodgates of unbelief upon the world.

The seventh-day Sabbath was given as a memorial to God's re-creative, sanctifying power. The prophet Ezekiel transmits these words of the Almighty Himself: "Moreover also I gave them my sabbaths, to be a sign between me and them, that they might know that I am the Lord that sanctify them." Ezekiel 20:12.

The same power of God is required to re-create and sanctify a sinful heart as was required to make man in the beginning. When we observe God's Sabbath, Ezekiel points out, we acknowledge Him as both Creator and Redeemer.

A friend of mine in Rhodesia called on the employer of a young African who had begun to observe the Biblical Sabbath.

"Some time ago," the employer said, "I noted a change in Samuel's life. At first I thought it would be very short-lived. But the transformation continued. Samuel has been a totally different person since he was converted and began observing the Sabbath. His conduct impressed me so much that I found an old Bible and began to read it. When I look at his life, somehow I have faith in Christianity again."

In Samuel's life the Sabbath became a sign of his re-creation—his new-birth experience.

*Thursday*

## Christ's Relation to the Sabbath

Not only did Jesus establish the seventh-day Sabbath during the first week of creation, but He observed it throughout His earthly ministry. This is not surprising, for Paul declares Him to be "the same yesterday, and to day, and for ever." (Hebrews 13:8.) He was called "Lord also of the sabbath." (Mark 2:28.)

"If ye love me," Jesus said, "keep my commandments." (John 14:15.) One of those commands reads, "Remember the sabbath day, to keep it holy.

Six days shalt thou labour, and do all thy work: but the seventh day is the sabbath of the Lord thy God: in it thou shalt not do any work." Exodus 20:8-10.

Jesus also lived what He taught. He "came down to Capernaum, a city of Galilee, and taught them on the sabbath days." (Luke 4:31.) Again, "He came to Nazareth, where he had been brought up: and, as his custom was, he went into the synagogue on the sabbath day, and stood up for to read." Luke 4:16.

Worshiping on the Sabbath was a regular custom with the Saviour. In precept and example He placed His seal of approval upon Sabbath observance, "leaving . . . an example, that ye should follow his steps." (1 Peter 2:21.)

Even in death the Saviour rested upon "the sabbath day according to the commandment." (Luke 23:56.) All of us know that Christ rose from the dead on the first day of the week—"Easter" Sunday. Jesus rested in the tomb on the day before Sunday —"the sabbath day according to the commandment"—commonly known today as Saturday. The Sabbath Christ kept during His earthly ministry has never lost its weekly identity through the centuries. That the Jews still keep it on Saturday proves that it has never been misplaced in the order of the week days.

It is a blessed experience to follow Jesus.

*Friday*

# Sabbath Observance Among the Disciples

After the Lord of the Sabbath laid down His life and was resting in the tomb, what did His disciples—those who were nearest to Him in His life of labor for others—do during the hours of the Sabbath following the crucifixion? Luke has recorded part of the answer to this question:

"It was Friday, and the Sabbath was about to begin. The women who had accompanied him from Galilee followed; they took note of the tomb and observed how his body was laid. Then they went home and prepared spices and perfumes; and on the Sabbath they rested in obedience to the commandment. But on the Sunday morning very early they came to the tomb bringing the spices they had prepared." Luke 23:54-56; 24:1, New English Bible. Following the example of Christ, they "rested the sabbath day according to the commandment."

But when Jesus returned to heaven after finishing His earthly ministry, and the years passed, did His followers observe the Sabbath? Fourteen years after the resurrection, Paul was preaching in the synagogues on the seventh-day Sabbath as his Master had done before him. (Acts 13:42-44.) "Paul, as his manner was, went in unto them, and three sabbath days reasoned with them out of the scriptures." Acts 17:2. "He reasoned in the synagogue every sabbath." "And he continued there a year and six months, teaching the word of God among them." Acts 18:4, 11. Thus we have a record of nearly eighty Sabbaths which Paul kept many years after the Saviour's resurrection.

Sixty years after Christ's ascension John the beloved spoke of "the Lord's day." (Revelation 1: 10.) Which day is the Lord's day in Scripture? In Mark 2:28 Jesus is called "Lord also of the sabbath," and Isaiah termed the Sabbath God's "holy day" (Isaiah 58:13).

Such followers of Jesus as Paul and others knew only one rest day, the seventh-day Sabbath embodied in the Ten Commandment law of God.

*Saturday*

# Was the Sabbath Changed?

Many Christians today believe that the Sabbath was changed from the seventh to the first day of the week. Here is a statement on this problem by one such individual:

"After the resurrection, we find the followers of

our Lord doing all that believers in God did on the Sabbath day and more, . . . but now they are meeting on the first day of the week. *The Scriptures of the New Testament are filled with such references.*"
—Samuel A. Jeanes, General Secretary of the Lord's Day Alliance of New Jersey, quoted in *These Times,* May, 1967.

Jeanes's organization is dedicated to more faithful Sunday observance. In what we must accept as an honest effort to base his appeal on God's Word, he states, *"The Scriptures . . . are filled with such references."*

If Christ or His followers changed the sacredness of the Sabbath from Saturday, the seventh day, to Sunday, the first day of the week, writers of the New Testament would certainly have made this clear and given reason for such an important change.

When the Passover celebration of the Jewish ceremonial law was replaced among the followers of Christ by the Lord's Supper, more commonly known today as the Communion service, both Jesus and the disciples left a clear record of the change so that there would be no question about it in the infant church or in the ranks of Christians in succeeding generations. (See Matthew 26:26; Mark 14:22; 1 Corinthians 10:16; 11:23-29.)

If you and I are sincerely seeking to follow Jesus and the teachings of His Word, we should prayerfully study the New Testament scriptures referring to the first day of the week. If the Scriptures are indeed *"filled with such references"* to the followers of the Lord doing on the first day of the week all that believers in God had done previously on the Sabbath, we should know this and honestly bring our lives into harmony with this new pronouncement.

"He that saith he abideth in him ought himself also so to walk, even as he walked." 1 John 2:6.

*Sunday*

# The First-Day Texts

Are the Scriptures filled with references to observance of the first instead of the seventh day of the week?

The first day of the week is mentioned only eight times in the New Testament. The first five of these—Matthew 28:1; Mark 16:1, 2, 9; Luke 24: 1; John 20:1—are merely factual accounts of what took place in connection with the thrilling resurrection of Christ on "the first day of the week." No reference is made in any of these passages to a change of the Sabbath.

In John 20:19 the apostle tells us that the disci-

ples were together on the first day of the week, not
for the purpose of a religious gathering but "for
fear of the Jews."

The author of the Book of Acts records a meeting on "the first day of the week, when the disciples
came together to break bread." (Acts 20:7.) Does
this prove that the followers of Jesus were observing
a new rest day set aside by their Master? Notice the
text more closely. Paul was on his third missionary
journey. The people of Troas wanted to hear him
preach, and because his boat was to sail from a
nearby port, they called an evening service. This
"breaking bread" was not part of the Communion
service, nor did it automatically make the day on
which it was broken a holy day, for in Acts 2:46 we
read, "And they, continuing *daily* with one accord
in the temple, and breaking bread from house to
house, did eat their meat with gladness and single-
ness of heart."

The last reference to the first day of the week is
in 1 Corinthians 16:2. This was no religious service.
Rather, Paul was calling for the believers to put
aside money *in their own homes* for the poor in
Jerusalem.

Do any of these texts suggest that the Sabbath of
the Lord was to be changed from Saturday, the
seventh day, to Sunday, the first day of the week,
in honor of the resurrection?

*Monday*

# How Was the Sabbath Changed?

If Christ and His followers did not change the Sabbath, how then did the "change" come about? The Roman Catholic Church answers the question for us:

"The [Catholic] Church changed the observance of the Sabbath to Sunday by right of the divine, infallible authority given to her by her Founder, Jesus Christ. The Protestant, claiming the Bible to be the only guide of faith, has no warrant for observing Sunday. In this matter the Seventh Day Adventist is the only consistent Protestant."—"The Question Box," *The Catholic Universe Bulletin,* August 14, 1942, p. 4.

Eusebius, one of the Church Fathers, wrote about the "change": "All things whatsoever that it was duty to do on the Sabbath, these we have transferred to the Lord's day."—*Commentary on the Psalms,* Eusebius, cited in *Commentary on the Apocalypse,* Moses Stuart, Vol. 2, p. 40.

Under the heading, "Change of the Sabbath," one Catholic Catechism contains this interesting material:

"*Question:* Which is the Sabbath day?

"*Answer:* Saturday is the Sabbath day.

"*Question:* Why do we observe Sunday instead of Saturday?

"*Answer:* We observe Sunday instead of Saturday because the Catholic Church transferred the solemnity from Saturday to Sunday."—Peter Geiermann, *The Convert's Catechism of Catholic Doctrine* (1957 ed.), p. 50.

Centuries ago Daniel the prophet was shown in vision the rise of a power which would "think to change times and laws." (Daniel 7:25.) We should not, then, be surprised when the papal power appears on the stage of action and confirms that it was, indeed, the Catholic Church that has "thought to change" God's law—His Ten Commandments, including God's seventh-day Sabbath.

*Tuesday*

# Views of Other Churchmen on the Sabbath

Many clergymen from churches which observe the first day of the week freely agree that there are no Bible grounds for Sunday observance.

James Cardinal Gibbons wrote, "You may read the Bible from Genesis to Revelation, and you will not find a single line authorizing the sanctification of Sunday. The scriptures enforce the religious observance of Saturday, a day which we never sanctify."—*The Faith of Our Fathers* (92d ed., rev.), p. 89.

The following interesting report appeared in a Canadian newspaper: "Rev. Philip Carrington, Anglican Archbishop of Quebec, sent local clergymen into a huddle today by saying outright that there was nothing to support Sunday being kept holy.

"Carrington defiantly told a church meeting in this city of straight-laced protestantism that tradition, not the Bible, had made Sunday the day of worship.

"He quoted the biblical commandment which said the seventh day should be one of rest, and then stated: 'That is Saturday.'

" 'Nowhere in the Bible is it laid down that worship should be done on Sunday,' the Archbishop told a hushed, still audience.

"Local parsons read his comments today with set, determined looks. They refused comment."— News item, *Albertan* (Calgary, Alberta, Canada), October 28, 1949.

What Alexander Campbell, founder of the 2,000,000-member Disciples of Christ Church, wrote is of interest: " 'But,' say some, 'it [the Sabbath] was *changed* from the seventh to the first day.' Where? when? and by whom? No man can tell. No, it was

7

never changed, nor could it be, unless creation was to be gone through again: for the reason assigned must be changed before the observance, or respect to the reason, can be changed!! It is all old wives' fables to talk of the change of the sabbath from the seventh to the first day."—*The Christian Baptist,* February 2, 1824.

Worth thinking about!

*Wednesday*

# Which Is Safe, Scripture or Tradition?

When we face a decision whether to accept the Holy Scriptures or man's tradition as a source of religious authority, what should our decision be? When Peter and the other apostles faced this question before the Jewish Council in Jerusalem, they knew the answer, even though it meant imprisonment and suffering, perhaps even death itself: "We ought to obey God rather than men." Acts 5:29.

It took real courage for Peter and his friends to take such a stand before this group of powerful men who had sentenced Christ to death but a short time before. They did not ask, "Is it a safe course for us to pursue? Will this decision cost us our lives?" They asked only, "Is this what God wants us to do?" Once this question was answered, their course was clear. They would obey God.

Through the centuries, following Christ has not always been easy. The majority of people have often misunderstood spiritual matters. It was so in Noah's day, in Abraham's, during Christ's earthly ministry, and during the time of the Reformation.

The Scriptures state, "Strait is the gate, and narrow is the way, which leadeth unto life, and few there be that find it." Matthew 7:14. We must not expect the majority to be willing to pay the price required in following Christ.

The narrow way may not be the popular way, but it is the only safe way, for Jesus warns, "Howbeit in vain do they worship me, teaching for doctrines the commandments of men." Mark 7:7. For "every plant, which my heavenly Father hath not planted, shall be rooted up." (Matthew 15:13.)

*Thursday*

# Promises and Performance

These words were written in describing Abraham's experience on Mount Moriah: "And Abraham called the name of that place Jehovah-jireh: as it is said to this day, In the mount of the Lord it

shall be seen." Genesis 22:14. Another translation
of the Bible records the last few words of our text:
"In the mountain of Yahweh [Jehovah] will provision be made." (Rotherham.) *Jehovah-jireh* means
"the Lord will provide."

What the old patriarch was told to do that day
appeared impossible. God commanded him to offer
his only son Isaac as a sacrifice on the mountain.
The old man went on the long, heartbreaking journey in obedience to that command, and though
there seemed nothing but darkness ahead, Abraham
believed that God would show him what to do. At
the moment of extremity the Lord sent a ram to replace Isaac as a sacrifice (Genesis 22:11-14), and
thus God honored Abraham's faith and his obedience in what, humanly speaking, appeared to be an
impossible situation.

Today the Lord is still *Jehovah-jireh* to all who
trust Him and obey His voice. He is able to provide
for the needs of His twentieth-century children just
as surely as He did for Abraham and Isaac. When
He speaks, we have only to obey Him. We must not
question His willingness or His capacity to meet our
particular problems.

"Our heavenly Father has a thousand ways to
provide for us of which we know nothing. Those
who accept the one principle of making the service
of God supreme, will find perplexities vanish and a

plain path before their feet. . . . He watches over His children with a love that is measureless and ever-lasting."—*The Ministry of Healing,* pp. 481, 482.

*Friday*

# God Honors the Obedient

Bill Manley, a construction worker who kept the seventh-day Sabbath, had just started a new job. He worked hard and well, and his plates, his studdings, his rafters—whatever he made—he fashioned with utmost skill and thoroughness. He worked with a silent prayer that God would help him be a good craftsman.

On Wednesday Bill went to his new employer before quitting time to tell him that he would not be at work on Saturday.

"Mr. Lawson," Bill began, "I keep the Sabbath, so I can't be here to work on Saturday. I have worked three days for you now. You have seen my work and can decide whether you want to continue my employment despite the inconvenience of my being off on Saturday. I'd very much like to work for you. But if my work isn't satisfactory, you still have two or three days to find someone to take my place before Saturday."

Mr. Lawson scratched his head and said, "Well,

Bill, you are a bit out of kilter with the world, but you have done good work and you have been fair in letting me know. We pay every Saturday noon. I'll just put your check in your toolbox, and you can get it anytime you want to after your Sabbath."

Bill honored God by obeying His commandments, by keeping the Sabbath. God honored Bill by helping him do top-quality work and by helping him to always have work with his Sabbaths free. Like Bill, we can depend upon God to do His part when we do ours. Just trust Him!

*Saturday*

# Faithfulness Is Required

Ben and Fred operated a service station in Lodi, California. For years the two men had been Sabbathkeepers, but since the oil company insisted that the station be open seven days a week, the two hired another man to operate the business on Saturday. Business dwindled. A regional company official investigated.

"You are not loyal Sabbathkeepers," he said. "If you were, you would not operate the station on Saturday." After giving the men some counsel on faithfulness, he took away their franchise.

The two new operators were also Sabbathkeepers, but they closed the station every Saturday, and their business prospered. Many months later the regional manager called. "You have certainly proved God!" he said. "Your sales for six days a week have far surpassed the highest sales of the station when it was open seven days."

Later the district manager accompanied the regional official in an inspection visit to the area and expressed his appreciation for the improved appearance of the station.

"These men keep the station open only six days a week," the district manager informed him.

"They can't do that," the higher official declared. "Our stations must be open seven days a week."

Sales records were produced, and the regional man was satisfied. "If it works like that, we had better let all our men do as they do," he decided.

Mary Ewing, of Louisville, Kentucky, was a secretary for an important firm. For five years she struggled with her conscience over the Sabbath question.

"I'm sure my boss will never let me have Saturday off," she kept telling herself.

Finally she could go on no longer, and she wrote a letter of resignation in shorthand and was sitting at her typewriter transcribing it when her boss walked in.

"Miss Ewing," he began, "we have decided to close the office on Saturdays. We are going on a five-day week."

For this secretary who had at last decided to obey God, this passage of Scripture took on real meaning: "And it shall come to pass, that before they call, I will answer; and while they are yet speaking, I will hear." Isaiah 65:24.

Whether we are in our own business or employed in the service of others, God honors faithfulness. There are over two million seventh-day-Sabbath-keeping Christians around the world, and God never fails to fulfill His promise to help when they bring their lives into harmony with His will.

*Sunday*

# Promises Which Do Not Fail

It is well for us to frequently refresh in our minds the never-failing promises of God. The Apostle Peter calls them "exceeding great and precious promises." (2 Peter 1:4.) These promises are designed to help you and me as we try to serve God each day.

When you face some overwhelming crisis, remember this verse: "When thou passest through the waters, I will be with thee; and through the rivers, they shall not overflow thee: when thou walkest through the fire, thou shalt not be burned; neither shall the flame kindle upon thee." Isaiah 43:2.

When you wonder whether God cares enough to provide the necessities of life, read, "I have been young, and now am old; yet have I not seen the righteous forsaken, nor his seed begging bread." Psalm 37:25.

"Beloved, I wish above all things that thou mayest prosper and be in health, even as thy soul prospereth." 3 John 2.

The Lord is mindful of your every need whether it be spiritual, temporal, or physical. He is as much concerned about your temporal and physical prosperity as He is about your spiritual welfare.

God does not promise that we will have all the luxuries of life, but the necessities are certain. "He shall dwell on high: his place of defence shall be the munitions of rocks: bread shall be given him; his waters shall be sure." Isaiah 33:16.

If we make God first in our lives, He makes Himself responsible for all our needs. Jesus pointed this out: "But seek ye first the kingdom of God, and his righteousness; and all these things shall be added unto you." Matthew 6:33.

Thus we can rest assured that God will keep His promises—if we let Him.

# SECTION IX

# After Life, the Judgment

Charles G. Finney, one of the great preachers of his day, had not always been a Christian. In his early days he was an unbelieving law student. An encounter with a Christian professor changed the whole course of his life.

"Tell me, Charles," the old professor began, "what are you going to do when you complete your studies?"

"Well," the young man replied, "I will put out my shingle and practice law."

"Yes," his friend continued, "and then what?"

"I suppose," Finney said, looking into the future, "I will build up a reputation, and I hope to make lots of money."

"Yes," his friend pursued, "and then what?"

"Oh, I'll build a beautiful home. I'll have a family and occupy a respected place in my community."

"Yes," the professor said, "and then what?"

"Why, I suppose I will eventually grow old and retire," Finney replied.

"Yes," his friend continued, "and then what?"

The youth was a bit perturbed but answered good-naturedly, "Oh, I'll grow old and die!"

"Yes, and then what?"

Finney had come to the end of his thinking, his planning. Beyond death there was nothing for him.

For days the urgent words, "And then what?" kept haunting him. He thought he had planned for everything, but he realized that he had failed to plan for the most important thing of all—eternity.

Finney remembered a Bible verse he had learned in childhood: "It is appointed unto men once to die, but after this the judgment." Hebrews 9:27. The thought of judgment led Charles Finney to feel his need and to dedicate his life to Christ.

*Tuesday*

## All Men Face the Judgment

Jesus believed in and taught that there is a judgment to come for all men. Of some cities in His own generation the Saviour said, "It shall be more tolerable for Tyre and Sidon at the day of judgment, than for you." Matthew 11:22. "The men of Nineveh shall rise in judgment with this generation, and shall condemn it," He declared on another occasion. (Matthew 12:41.) In verse 42 He warns, "The queen of the south shall rise up in judgment with this generation, and shall condemn it," because of its unbelief.

In John 5:27 Christ reminds us that the Father

"hath given him authority to execute judgment also, because he is the Son of man." Also in the fifth and seventh chapters of Matthew, the Saviour speaks of the day of judgment and warns men to beware of that day. We may study the judgment with assurance that Jesus, our great Example, believed in and taught the judgment.

The prophet Daniel gives an inspired account of the great judgment scene that we shall consider shortly. Jesus specifies that Daniel's book is one we should read and understand: "When ye therefore shall see the abomination of desolation, spoken of by Daniel the prophet, stand in the holy place, (whoso readeth, let him understand)." Matthew 24:15.

We shall study together the inspired description of the judgment scene in heaven set forth by Daniel. Jesus said that we should read and understand it. With the guidance of the Holy Spirit, let us do just this.

*Wednesday*

# Record Books in Heaven

Daniel wrote about certain books being opened at the time of judgment. One of these books is the book of life, which John mentions in Revelation 20:

12: "I saw the dead, small and great, stand before God; and the books were opened: and another book was opened, which is the book of life." In this book of life have been written the names of all the human race since Adam's day who have been adopted into the family of God.

Another book of judgment is spoken of as the book of remembrance. In this book, the prophet Malachi asserts, have been recorded the good deeds of all who feared God and thought often upon His name. (Malachi 3:16.) Every generous and thoughtful deed, every kind word, every tender thought, has been carefully entered by the angels of God in the book of remembrance. Every temptation resisted, every evil overcome, has been faithfully recorded. Every little act of self-sacrifice made for Christ's sake, every trial patiently endured for Him, has been written by angel hands and will come up in remembrance before the Father when our names are called.

*Thursday*

# Eavesdropping by Remote Control

A news story in *The New York Times* describes various electronic eavesdropping devices presented before a Senate investigating committee. The manufacturer revealed that equipment has now been so perfected that a private conversation in the nation's capital can be monitored in Hawaii.

"The long-range listening device was demonstrated by Emanuel Mittleman, who operates the Wireless Guitar Company in Brooklyn, N.Y.

"He said the device could be attached to a telephone line and could be used to monitor a conversation in a room from any place that could be reached by direct dialing on the telephone.

"Once the device is installed, the snooper merely calls the number of the telephone to which it is attached. From then on he can hear all conversations in the room, even though the telephone is hung up. The device derives its operating power from the telephone line, he said."

"Other devices displayed, and in some cases demonstrated, included microphones concealed in the olive in a martini, in a tie clasp, in a package of cigarettes, in a picture frame, in a cigarette lighter and in a woman's purse."—*The New York Times,* February 19, 1965.

If man with his finite limitations can devise such phenomenal devices to transmit and record, then "can any hide himself in secret places that I shall not see him?" asks the Lord. (Jeremiah 23:24.) "The Lord looketh from heaven; he beholdeth all the sons of men." Psalm 33:13.

Is man capable of doing some things that God cannot do?

*Friday*

# Laser Beam Eavesdropping

"A laser beam device is being developed that will pick up conversations inside an office via the vibrations of voices bounding off the office's windows, explained Bernard Fensterwald, counsel to Senator Edward V. Long's Judiciary Subcommittee on Administrative Practice.

"The beam could be aimed from a location blocks away from the target office and bounced off the window to pick up the sound vibrations, Fensterwald told a meeting of Electronics Industries Association members."—Washington *Post,* March 16, 1967.

With man-made eavesdropping devices such as this, we have little reason to question God's ability to see, to hear, and to record all our words, thoughts, and actions in His book of judgment.

"God shall bring every work into judgment," the inspired Word informs us, "with every secret thing, whether it be good, or whether it be evil." Ecclesiastes 12:14.

"He [man] may have committed his evil deeds

in the light of day or in the darkness of night; but they were open and manifest before Him with whom we have to do. Angels of God witnessed each sin, and registered it in the unerring records. Sin may be concealed, denied, covered up from father, mother, wife, children, and associates; no one but the guilty actors may cherish the least suspicion of the wrong; but it is laid bare before the intelligences of heaven. The darkness of the darkest night, the secrecy of all deceptive arts, is not sufficient to veil one thought from the knowledge of the Eternal. God has an exact record of every unjust account and every unfair dealing."—*The Great Controversy,* p. 486.

Are you prepared for such scrutiny?

*Saturday*

# Cramming for the Finals

"Grandma, why are you always reading your Bible?" a youngster demanded one day. "Every time I see you, you are reading it!"

The old lady smiled and replied thoughtfully, "Well, honey, you might say I'm cramming for my final examination."

"Cramming for my final examination"—there is food for thought for each one of us in those words. We must all face the judgment, the great final ex-

amination day, and it is well that we should begin
preparing now.

What will be God's standard on that final examination day? "Let us hear the conclusion of the whole
matter: Fear God, and keep his commandments:
for this is the whole duty of man." Ecclesiastes
12:13.

We should not be surprised that in God's court-
room, the law of God—His Ten Commandments—
is the standard by which men are judged. The laws
of California are used in California's courtrooms.
British law decides cases in United Kingdom courts.
"We shall all be judged one day, not by each other's
standards or even our own, but by the standard of
Christ." Romans 14:10, Phillips.

"So speak ye, and so do, as they that shall be
judged by the law of liberty." James 2:12. If you
wish to be certain which law James is referring to,
read verses 11 and 10: "For he that said, Do not
commit adultery, said also, Do not kill. Now if thou
commit no adultery, yet if thou kill, thou art become
a transgressor of the law." "For whosoever shall
keep the whole law, and yet offend in one point,
he is guilty of all."

Probably all of us would do well to spend more
time with our Bibles, "cramming for final examination." Life is one course which—should we fail
the final test—we can't take over.

*Sunday*

# Man's Advocate

We have been dwelling on solemn thoughts. The judgment is indeed an awe-inspiring subject, and I am grateful that we do not have to face the prospect of judgment alone. Jesus will be there to represent all who will permit Him to do so.

To think of standing before a holy God unrepresented strikes the poor human heart with terror, but to be assured that Jesus is there to plead for us changes the picture completely. He has been on earth as a man among men. He has met the same tests and trials and temptations we have to meet. He is well acquainted with the weakness of human flesh; therefore, in a sympathetic and understanding manner, He is able to present our cases before the heavenly Judge.

"My little children, these things write I unto you, that ye sin not. And if any man sin, we have an advocate with the Father, Jesus Christ the righteous." 1 John 2:1.

When my name is called and my life weighed in the balance of the Ten Commandments as Holy Scripture says it will be (Ecclesiastes 12:13, 14), Jesus as my Attorney will plead for me if I permit Him. If every sin has been confessed and forgiven,

He will say to God, "Father, I know this man was a
sinner; he does not deserve to live, but he has confessed his sins, and I have forgiven them. He stood
for Me down there on earth, and now I stand for
him. He is Mine, Father; I have graven him upon
the palms of My hands. For My sake blot out his
sins, and retain his name in the book of life. My
blood covers his life of sin." (See Matthew 10:32,
Isaiah 49:16, and John 17:24.)

Thus it is that Jesus, as my Advocate, will plead
for me before the judgment bar of God if I have
accepted Him and asked Him to forgive my every
sin and cover me with His precious blood. Because
of His appeal on my behalf, the Father accepts me as
a joint heir with Christ, and my name is retained in
the book of life. (Revelation 3:5.)

*Monday*

# The Required Preparation

What of those who have taken the name of the
Lord, making a profession of Christ but later bringing reproach and shame upon the Christian faith by
reverting to a life of sin? Of such Jesus declares, "I
never knew you." Matthew 7:23. If we are guilty of
such conduct, our good deeds will be erased from
the book of remembrance (Ezekiel 18:24), and our

names blotted forever from the book of life kept in heaven.

Have you placed *your* case in the hands of Jesus? Is He your Advocate before the bar of God? This work of judgment has been going on in the heavenly sanctuary for many years now. How soon the cases of the dead will be finished and work begun on the cases of the living, we do not know.

It may have already reached that phase, but we have no way of knowing this. "Silently, unnoticed as the midnight thief, will come the decisive hour which marks the fixing of every man's destiny." You may be at work, in your home, traveling on the highway, or shopping in some store, when *your* name is called. You will not be aware that the final irrevocable decision has been pronounced, sealing your fate for eternity. Can you truthfully say, "I am ready"?

*Tuesday*

# When Does the Judgment Begin?

The Scriptures state that God has set a time for the judgment of the world: "He hath appointed a day, in the which he will judge the world in righteousness." Acts 17:31.

In Revelation 14:14-16 John creates an inspired picture of the second coming of Christ: "And I looked, and behold a white cloud, and upon the cloud one sat like unto the Son of man, having on his head a golden crown, and in his hand a sharp sickle. And another angel came out of the temple, crying with a loud voice to him that sat on the cloud, Thrust in thy sickle, and reap: for the time is come for thee to reap; for the harvest of the earth is ripe. And he that sat on the cloud thrust in his sickle on the earth; and the earth was reaped."

Immediately prior to the Saviour's glorious appearing, all men are to be warned of the final judgment, as these verses in Revelation indicate: "And I saw another angel fly in the midst of heaven, having the everlasting gospel to preach unto them that dwell on the earth, and to every nation, and kindred, and tongue, and people, saying with a loud voice, Fear God, and give glory to him; for the hour of his judgment is come: and worship him that made heaven, and earth, and the sea, and the fountains of waters." Revelation 14:6, 7.

Note that the statement is that "the hour of his judgment *is* come." The inspired writer did not say that the hour of His judgment *will* come, but rather uses the present tense "*is* come."

The time of judgment will be characterized by great religious apostasy, a time when men will have forgotten their Creator and their Redeemer. It will be a time when men are exulting in their own achievements rather than recognizing God. The message of Revelation challenges mankind to "fear God, and give glory to him."

Another clue to the time of the judgment is found in Revelation 11:18: "And the nations were angry, and thy wrath is come, and the time of the dead, that they should be judged." The judgment will be in session when the nations are angry, a time when God will "destroy them which destroy the earth."

Surely we are living in the days of God's judgment, and that message proclaiming, "The hour of his judgment *is* come," *is* being disseminated throughout the world "to every nation, and kindred, and tongue, and people." (Revelation 14:6.)

# SECTION X

*Wednesday*

# One With a Hundred Zeros
## After It

You don't know what a one with a hundred zeros after it is called? Well, as a matter of fact, I don't either, and it really doesn't matter a great deal. But it matters to millions of non-Christians in certain parts of the Orient. They believe Paradise is reached only after an individual has passed through as many worlds as would be numbered by the figure one with one hundred Zeros after it.

The length of such a "world"? This is interesting also. The length of their "world" is as long as it would take to rub Mount Everest out of existence by going once every hundred years and giving it a few brushes with a piece of cotton. Quite a formidable—and interminable—task, isn't it? But wait, you aren't in Paradise yet.

After the "soul" has spent a near eternity obliterating Mount Everest, you would think his entrance into Paradise assured. But after all this effort his chance of getting in is only as great as the chance of making two needles balance point to point by holding one above the other and dropping the upper one toward the lower. Not much hope here—yet there are millions of people who have such a concept of "heaven," or the reward of righteous beings.

Man's concept of "heaven" is probably as varied as the branches of religion in the world. The American Indian was buried with his bow and arrows and his favorite horse, so that he could enjoy his trip to a happy hunting ground. In the museum at Cairo, Egypt, where the mummy of King Tutankhamen is kept, there is a royal couch, a chariot of gold, and elaborate furniture of all descriptions, all of which had been placed in the king's tomb to make him happy when he reached the mystic land of Egyptian mythology.

But really, what *is* "over there"?

*Thursday*

# "Heaven Doesn't Matter"?

To many Christians heaven is a vague, faraway place in which a vaporlike body will float aimlessly about the "Beautiful Isle of Somewhere," strumming a harp. Little wonder an article appeared in a popular American magazine under the title, "Heaven Doesn't Matter." Commenting on the harp and cloud-bank concept of heaven, the author confessed honestly, "I've never been able to get very excited over heaven myself."

I am afraid I couldn't get very excited about that kind of heaven either. I like action. I like going places and doing things. I like real people. I love the beautiful mountains, the clear lakes. I found great pleasure in Africa visiting the game parks and watching the elephants, the antelopes, the lions, and all of the other animals. The Bible assures me that heaven is going to be a very real place.

The Word of God reveals that this world of sin will be purified by fire, "wherein the heavens being on fire shall be dissolved, and the elements shall melt with fervent heat." (2 Peter 3:12.) There will then come forth from God's hand a renewed creation, restored to pristine Edenic splendor. "For, behold, I create new heavens and a new earth: and the former shall not be remembered, nor come into mind." Isaiah 65:17.

"Behold, I create new heavens and a new earth." God must be calling someone's attention to His work of a new creation! In our day we do not say, "Behold!" when we wish someone to notice what we are doing. We usually say "Watch" or "Look here." Could it be that the redeemed ones of earth will have the privilege of watching God perform His re-creative act after the world has been purified by fire? It is a stimulating thought. I would like to witness such a scene—God creating new heavens and a new earth.

*Friday*

# Heaven Is a Real Place

A Dutchman leaving an evangelistic meeting paused to express appreciation for the evangelist's presentation of the "Home of the Saved." The evangelist had been stressing the reality of heaven.

"I vould radder be somebody going someplace und knows ven I gets der dan to be nobody going no place und knowing nudding ven I gets der!"

Our Dutch friend with his broken English had something! He spoke words worthy of our consideration!

Heaven is, indeed, a real place. Jesus declares it to be so. "In my Father's house are many mansions: if it were not so, I would have told you. I go to prepare *a place* for you. And if I go and prepare *a place* for you, I will come again, and receive you unto myself; that where I am, there ye may be also." John 14:2, 3.

Twice in this passage the Saviour promised His disciples He would prepare *a place* for them. According to the dictionary a "place" has physical environment, physical surroundings, or both. The same authority declares "place" to be "a particular part of a surface or body."—*Webster's New Collegiate Dictionary,* Seventh Edition.

So when Jesus said that He went to prepare a place—a very real place—He meant just what He said. It is not all clouds and spirits and glory. It will have "physical environment and physical surroundings with a real surface or body."

The Word of God describes real trees that will be there. "Instead of the thorn shall come up the fir tree, and instead of the brier shall come up the myrtle tree." Isaiah 55:13. There are real animals there. "The wolf and the lamb shall feed together, and the lion shall eat straw like the bullock." Isaiah 65:25. Real flowers will be there. "And the desert shall rejoice, and blossom as the rose. It shall blossom abundantly." Isaiah 35:1, 2. There will be real houses and real gardens there. "They shall build houses, and inhabit them; and they shall plant vineyards, and eat the fruit of them." Isaiah 65:21. Real mansions will be there. "In my Father's house are many mansions." John 14:2. A beautiful river— real and crystal clear—will flow "out of the throne of God." (Revelation 22:1.) There will be real fruit from real trees for real people to eat. "In the midst of the street of it, and on either side of the river, was there the tree of life, which bare twelve manner of fruits, and yielded her fruit every month." Revelation 22:2.

Thank God that heaven is a real place with real things and real people.

*Saturday*

# No Idlers in Heaven

If you have conceived of heaven as an idle man's paradise, you are wrong. Heaven will be a place of activity. Of those who become heaven's inhabitants the Scriptures state, "They shall build houses, and inhabit them; and they shall plant vineyards, and eat the fruit of them." Isaiah 65:21.

In this present life misfortune often overtakes us; in a moment the work of a lifetime is swept from our grasp, and the house of our dreams is lost. But in heaven there will be no crop failures, no mortgage foreclosures. "They shall not build, and another inhabit; they shall not plant, and another eat: for as the days of a tree are the days of my people, and mine elect shall long enjoy the work of their hands. They shall not labour in vain, nor bring forth for trouble; for they are the seed of the blessed of the Lord, and their offspring with them." Verses 22, 23.

"The earth shall be full of the knowledge of the Lord, as the waters cover the sea." Isaiah 11:9.

Ellen G. White wrote:

"There every power will be developed, every capability increased. The grandest enterprises will be carried forward, the loftiest aspirations will be reached, the highest ambitions realized. And still there will arise new heights to surmount, new wonders to admire, new truths to comprehend, fresh objects to call forth the powers of body and mind and soul.

"All the treasures of the universe will be open to the study of God's children. With unutterable delight we shall enter into the joy and the wisdom of unfallen beings. We shall share the treasures gained through ages upon ages spent in contemplation of God's handiwork. And the years of eternity, as they roll, will continue to bring more glorious revelations."—*Education,* p. 307.

Do you want to grow gardens, build houses, do something beyond your present capacity? Are you frustrated with the limited time and abilities you have in this world? When the new earth is as "full of the knowledge of God as the waters cover the sea," you will be able to do anything your glorified mind desires—*that is, if you are there!*

*Sunday*

# No Sickness, No Death

I have seen thousands of sick persons and lepers, but I never get used to it. My pastor's heart ever goes out in tender sympathy to the unfortunate person who is overcome by disease and suffering.

The hospitals in all lands are full of tortured men and women suffering from headaches, backaches, twisted limbs, cramped chests, parched lips, and burning fevers. What a glorious day it would be if some great physician could appear and by a word forever banish all sickness and suffering. *That day will come.* God's Word declares it will be so—but not in our present world.

In the earth made new, according to the Scriptures, "the inhabitant shall not say, I am sick." (Isaiah 33:24.) "Then the eyes of the blind shall be opened, and the ears of the deaf shall be unstopped. Then shall the lame man leap as an hart, and the tongue of the dumb sing." Isaiah 35:5, 6.

Nearly everyone at some time has sat by the side of a loved one and watched him take those last few halting breaths and then slip into eternity. We have known the grief, the heartache, the loneliness that follow such an experience. In heaven there will be no more heartbreaks, no more agony, for "God shall wipe away all tears from their eyes, and there shall be no more death, neither sorrow, nor crying, neither shall there be any more pain: for the former things are passed away." (Revelation 21:4.)

Write it on the golden tablets of your heart! Tell it to your sorrowing friends! Shout it from the housetops—there will *never* again be any heartaches or heartbreaks in that painless, deathless, sorrowless world which has been promised to the redeemed.

*Monday*

# Will We Recognize Each Other?

"Aren't you the speaker on the Bible Auditorium of the Air broadcast over WHN?" The question startled me, for, after all, New York City has several million people, and out of all those millions how could the operator of a newsstand recognize me when I had merely asked for the evening paper?

"Oh, I listen to you every day," he explained, "and as soon as you opened your mouth I knew who you were."

Riding on a crowded subway another day I had a similar experience—I was recognized by my voice.

The Word of God suggests that in heaven we shall be known as we are known here in this life, possibly by those same characteristics which identify us here, such as our voices, and mannerisms; perhaps even our glorified bodies may retain at least some resemblance to our earthly ones.

Paul asserts, "For now we see through a glass, darkly; but then face to face: now I know in part; but then shall I know even as also I am known." 1 Corinthians 13:12.

8

Peter, James, and John recognized Moses and Elijah in their glorified bodies as they beheld them on the Mount of Transfiguration. In fact, they talked together. The story of this experience is found in Matthew 17:1-8.

Jesus, after His resurrection, in His glorified body, was recognized by Mary. "Jesus said to her, 'Why are you weeping? Who is it you are looking for?' Thinking it was the gardener, she said, 'If it is you, sir, who removed him, tell me where you have laid him, and I will take him away.' Jesus said, 'Mary!' She turned to him and said, 'Rabbuni!' (which is Hebrew for 'My Master')." John 20:15, 16, N.E.B.

The disciples on the way to Emmaus also recognized Christ after His resurrection. Could it have been by the manner in which He said grace? "And it came to pass, as he sat at meat with them, he took bread, and blessed it, and brake, and gave to them. And their eyes were opened, and they knew him." Luke 24:30, 31.

What it will be about us that people will recognize us by will probably vary from person to person. But whatever it will be, people will know us.

I am glad that in that better land we will recognize one another—our loved ones and friends who will be there. Indeed, "then shall I know even as also I am known."

*Tuesday*

# No Glass Between

A little London urchin was left in the care of a hard-drinking woman after his parents were killed in an accident. Beaten and cursed, the little fellow had to beg in the streets, and the only pleasure the child knew was "window shopping." He loved to look longingly in the windows and see the breathtaking toys, the warm clothes, the tempting sweets, the appetizing baked products, but *there was always a glass between!*

One day the child was struck by a car and badly injured. He was rushed to the hospital; and when he regained consciousness, he was in a clean bed with white sheets and he looked up into the pleasant face of a nurse. Though his frail body was racked with pain, he found the place strangely acceptable.

Days passed. The boy improved and was finally able to sit up. There by his bedside he discovered a large red box filled with multicolored toy soldiers and their equipment. He reached out his little hand toward the box. He could scarcely believe that there was no glass between his hand and the toys. The soldiers were his! Falteringly he whispered, "Is it really true—*there is no glass*—are they really mine?" A nod of the head and a smile on the nurse's face assured him that they were really his to keep.

Our human condition is somewhat like that of the little boy: "For now we see through a glass, darkly; but then face to face: now I know in part; but then shall I know even as also I am known." 1 Corinthians 13:12.

This life is filled with frustrations and disappointments. Too frequently, it seems, there is a glass between us and our hopes, our legitimate objectives, our fondest goals. Too many of the truly good things of life are beyond our reach. There is that ever-present "glass" between.

"Now we see through a glass darkly." One of these days when Jesus comes, the glass will be removed. We will see our Saviour face to face; the glories of the sinless new earth will be ours.

*Wednesday*

## "They Shall See His Face"

"When you get to heaven, Billy, what do you want to see most?" a Christian teacher asked one of her first-graders.

Billy thought a moment. There was much his little heart longed for. He had heard the blessed land with its beauties, its treasures, its delicacies, spoken of frequently.

"Please, teacher," the little fellow replied, "I want to see the lions, the mansions, and the angels, but most of all I want to see Jesus."

Fanny J. Crosby, the hymn writer, expresses the same longing in these words:

"Through the gates to the city, in a robe of spotless
    white,
  He will lead me where no tears shall ever fall;
  In the glad song of ages I shall mingle with delight;
  But I long to meet my Saviour first of all."

What Christian heart has not filled with the same desire? In the midst of life's turmoil and stresses have *you* not also longed to see your Saviour?

The precious promise to the redeemed is, "The throne of God and of the Lamb shall be in it; . . . *and they shall see his face.*" Revelation 22:3, 4.

Yes, Jesus will be there, and He "shall feed them, and shall lead them unto living fountains of waters." (Revelation 7:17.) We shall be like Him at His appearing (1 John 3:2), and we shall be with Him throughout the ages of eternity.

Of the redeemed, the author of Revelation says, "These are they which follow the Lamb whithersoever he goeth." Revelation 14:4. It was a wonderful privilege the disciples of Jesus enjoyed as they lived with Him during His three-year ministry on earth. They saw His mighty healing power. They listened to the words of life as they fell from His lips and penetrated their hearts.

The prospect before us is even more glorious. Not for three brief years will we be with Christ, but throughout eternity. The disciples were forced to witness His scourging and crucifixion. You and I may witness His coronation—His glorious rule as King of kings and Lord of lords. They had hoped to see Him end the iron rule of Rome. We will see Him end the reign of sin.

The disciples could follow Jesus over only a comparatively few square miles, but you and I have the prospect of following our Lord from planet to planet. We may follow Him "whithersoever he goeth."

There are some sobering facts that we must not lose sight of, some conditions for entry to heaven as outlined in this passage: "Blessed are the pure in heart: for they shall see God." Matthew 5:8. If we expect to see Him in the hereafter, our hearts must be pure here. The blood of the Lamb must cleanse our hearts *now* if we hope to see Him *then*. Sin must be confessed and forsaken. Only clean men and women can see, and have fellowship with, a holy Saviour.

If you and I expect to "follow the Lamb whithersoever he goeth" in the earth made new, we must begin following Him now in this earth.

*Thursday*

# What Eternity Is

"With unutterable delight the children of earth enter into the joy and the wisdom of unfallen beings. They share the treasures of knowledge and understanding gained through ages upon ages in contemplation of God's handiwork. With undimmed vision they gaze upon the glory of creation,—suns and stars and systems, all in their appointed order circling the throne of Deity. Upon all things, from the least to the greatest, the Creator's name is written, and in all are the riches of His power displayed.

"And the years of eternity, as they roll, will bring richer and still more glorious revelations of God and of Christ. As knowledge is progressive, so will love, reverence, and happiness increase. The more men learn of God, the greater will be their admiration of His character. As Jesus opens before them the riches of redemption, and the amazing achievements in the great controversy with Satan, the hearts of the ransomed thrill with more fervent devotion, and with more rapturous joy they sweep the harps of gold; and ten thousand times ten thousand and thousands of thousands of voices unite to swell the mighty chorus of praise.

" 'And every creature which is in heaven, and
on the earth, and under the earth, and such as are in
the sea, and all that are in them, heard I saying,
Blessing, and honor, and glory, and power, be unto
Him that sitteth upon the throne, and unto the
Lamb forever and ever.'

"The great controversy is ended. Sin and sinners
are no more. The entire universe is clean. One pulse
of harmony and gladness beats through the vast
creation. From Him who created all, flow life and
light and gladness, throughout the realms of illimita-
ble space. From the minutest atom to the greatest
world, all things, animate and inanimate, in their
unshadowed beauty and perfect joy, declare that
God is love."—*The Great Controversy,* pp. 677,
678.

*Friday*

# The Preparation Process

As you enter the city of Damascus by the street
called Straight, you may visit some of the shops
where Damascus brocade is produced. I was in-
trigued with what I saw there. The looms in the shop
were primitive but also quite complex. From the
pattern above the loom it seemed that thread was
streaming down in all directions to the shuttles.

To the uninitiated eye it just didn't make sense. But the skill of the weaver produced beautiful brocade. That maze of thread emerging from the overhead pattern produced, in the hands of the master weaver, a rich silk fabric with raised patterns in gold or silver.

There is also a pattern for every life. There are the golden threads of happiness, silver threads of accomplishment, crimson threads of satisfaction, blue threads of honor. There are also some gray threads of frustration, some black threads of heartache and sorrow.

But when the pattern of your role has been cast in heaven above and the hands of the Master Weaver skillfully ply the loom of your life, the results can be glorious. We may not understand at times why there are so many threads of heartache, so few of joy; but when we arrive safely on the other shore, we'll understand, and we would not want to be led in any other path than our Saviour has chosen for us.

"My life is but a weaving
Between my God and me.
I only chose the colors
He weaveth steadily.
Sometimes He weaveth sorrow,
And I in foolish pride

Forget He sees the upper
And I the lower side."

*—Author Unknown.*

God will weave into the fabric of our lives just enough dark threads to make a glorious brocade for eternity. "Here is the staggering thing—that in all which will one day belong to him we have been promised a share." Ephesians 1:11, Phillips. It will take the dark as well as the bright threads to make it ours!

# SECTION XI

*Saturday*

# A Wonderful Family

A fellow minister and I were flying from Salisbury, Rhodesia, to Nairobi, Kenya. We were not airborne long before a pleasant little woman came to our seats and greeted us.

"Pardon me, but aren't you Seventh-day Adventist ministers?"

We said we were.

"I was sure I had heard you speak down in South Africa."

After a brief visit she returned to her seat, and a few minutes later the stewardess handed us a note that read: "With those who have the same faith—the same hope—it is almost like being real brothers and sisters. The Adventist family is indeed a wonderful family to which to belong. May God bless you both."

*"A wonderful family to which to belong"*—I soon found myself in deep meditation. Actually, it *is* like belonging to a large family. There is something about "the blessed hope" of which Paul speaks in his letter to Timothy that indeed binds men and women of many lands together in bonds akin to those of a family.

The Apostle Paul, in his letter to the Christians

at Ephesus, speaks of those who belong to the Lord Jesus Christ as resembling a family: "For this cause I bow my knees unto the Father of our Lord Jesus Christ, of whom the whole family in heaven and earth is named." Ephesians 3:14, 15.

*"The whole family in heaven and earth"*—that's it—a blessed fellowship here and now and a precious association in a glorious hereafter. It is, indeed, a family on earth; it will be part of the family of God in heaven.

*Sunday*

# Ancestor Hunting

"Do you have any information about our ancestors?" a relative of mine once wrote. "I am working on a genealogy of our family on mother's side. Can you help me?" I am only one in thousands who have received a similar request. It is an avid pastime of many to trace their ancestors. Old court records, old Bibles, faded baptismal and dedication certificates, moss-covered tombstones, all are studied eagerly to discover information about ancestors. We must know who we are, where we came from. Many thousands of dollars are spent in the sometimes elusive game of ancestor hunting.

The follower of Christ will find the genealogy

of his spiritual ancestors in the third chapter of Luke's Gospel. Here, among an apparently endless list of "the son of's," one finds the human forebears of Christ on Joseph's side. They are all there—Nathan, David, Jacob, Isaac, Abraham, Noah, Methuselah, Enoch, and others amid a galaxy of God's heroes. The genealogy takes us back to the beginning: "Which was the son of Enos, which was the son of Seth, which was the son of Adam, which was the son of God." Luke 3:38.

"Which was the son of Adam, *which was the son of God*"—what a genealogy!

Unfortunately sin separated man from this relationship with the Creator. But, thank God, the connection may be restored through Jesus Christ our Lord and Saviour. "We are the children of God: and if children, then heirs; heirs of God, and joint-heirs with Christ." Romans 8:16, 17.

"Ye shall be my sons and daughters, saith the Lord Almighty." 2 Corinthians 6:18.

*Monday*

# Joining God's Family

When the disciples came to Jesus with the request that He teach them to pray, how did He instruct them to approach God?

"After this manner therefore pray ye," the Master said: *"Our Father which art in heaven."* Matthew 6:9.

Not as the omnipotent Deity did Christ instruct His followers to address their Creator. He was, and is, indeed, all powerful, but Jesus wanted the disciples then, as He desires us today, to know God by that most precious relationship—"our Father which art in heaven."

*"Our Father"*—what more tender appellation could we choose? "God can bestow no higher honor upon mortals than to adopt them into His family, giving them the privilege of calling Him Father."

With God as our Father, with Jesus Christ as our Elder Brother, with all who seek to walk in the footsteps of Jesus becoming brothers and sisters, what a family this is! Many times those who are brothers and sisters in Christ are closer to one another than are blood relatives.

"You are no longer outsiders or aliens, but fellow citizens with every other Christian—you belong now to the household of God." Ephesians 2:19, Phillips.

I am a father. I know how closely my two sons are bound to my own heart. Through the years the experiences my sons have had in facing problems have touched my own heart. If God's love for me is like a father's love, I can well understand it. If he loves me as a father, then such love is very real to me. I am no longer an alien; I am the son of His love, a cherished member of the family of God.

*Tuesday*

# A Family With a Mission

During the past thirty-five years I have traveled widely in the fifty states of America, in Canada, Europe, Asia, Africa, Australia, South and Central America, and the islands of the seas. There are not many countries I have not visited. The one thing that stands out in my contacts with these many lands is that in nearly every country I have found members of the church to which I belong, brothers and sisters in the faith, cherishing as I do the hope that our Lord's return will be soon.

Nearly twenty centuries ago the Saviour commanded, "Go ye into all the world, and preach the gospel to every creature." Mark 16:15. Following this divine commission, the disciples and members of the apostolic church fanned out over the known world of their day. In thirty years the gospel swept through Asia Minor, across eastern Europe, and into the city of Rome, the mistress of the world. In the face of bitter persecution, and often deadly opposition, the heralds of the cross, under the power of the

Holy Spirit, planted the ensign of the Crucified One upon the very doorsteps of the imperial household. Before he died, the Apostle Paul could report, "Mission accomplished." The gospel "was preached to every creature which is under heaven." (Colossians 1:23.)

Through succeeding centuries the Saviour's words have been ringing in the ears of His followers. Members of God's family must never be content to settle down and hoard the treasures of His grace in seclusion. They must share the good things of the kingdom with those about them, at home and in faraway lands.

God's family today is not an American family, not European, African, or Asian. It embraces the whole world, because modern followers of Christ have gone "into all the world" with the good news of a Saviour's death, resurrection, and soon return.

*Wednesday*

# An International Family

"And I saw another angel fly in the midst of heaven, having the everlasting gospel to preach unto them that dwell on the earth, and to every nation, and kindred, and tongue, and people." Revelation 14:6.

The gospel of the kingdom—the message of Christ's literal return to earth in the very near future —is a message for the whole world. It must, indeed, go to all "them that dwell on the earth, and to every nation, and kindred, and tongue, and people." Here is no evangel confined to one city, one state, one province, one nation, or even to one continent. The family of God is an international family. Its members are found almost everywhere.

Responding to the commission of Christ, accepting the challenge of an international ministry, the Adventist family has spread rapidly into many lands. The Seventh-day Adventist movement is not an old movement, as churches today measure their age. We find our roots in the fulfillment of Bible prophecy during the middle years of the past century. Ministers and laymen in different lands of America, Europe, and Asia began preaching the distinctive truths of prophetic interpretation that marked our beginnings.

Today Seventh-day Adventist work is found in most lands of earth. The United Nations lists some 226 countries and political subdivisions in the world. Seventh-day Adventists are carrying on their work in 190 of these. The population of the countries in which Adventists serve represents 98.46 percent of the peoples of the world.

But there is still a great work to be done.

*Thursday*

# The Worldwide Challenge

When Christ sent out His disciples, He said, "And as ye go, preach, saying, The kingdom of heaven is at hand." Matthew 10:7. In harmony with this instruction, Seventh-day Adventists have been "preaching, teaching, and healing" in many lands for many years.

Jesus said, "As ye go, preach." The Apostle Paul declared, "It pleased God by the foolishness of preaching to save them that believe." 1 Corinthians 1:21. The preaching ministry of Seventh-day Adventists is today being carried on by radio and television, through churches and public evangelistic missions, and through home and personal visitation in more than one thousand languages of earth. "The gospel of the kingdom" is a message which, like that of John the Baptist, will "make ready a people prepared for the Lord." (Luke 1:17.)

The Voice of Prophecy radiobroadcast, with H. M. S. Richards as the speaker in English, is now heard in nine languages. Faith for Today and It Is Written telecasts, featuring W. A. Fagal and George Vandeman, are seen daily or weekly in many lands. If you are interested in enrolling in a course of Bible study, write to The Voice of Prophecy, Box 55, Los

Angeles, California 90053; Faith for Today, Box 8, New York, New York 10008; or General Conference of Seventh-day Adventists, 6840 Eastern Avenue, N.W., Washington, D.C. 20012, and ask to be enrolled in a free Bible Correspondence Course.

In response to the Saviour's command to "heal the sick," twenty-one thousand full-time employees are today operating 135 Seventh-day Adventist hospitals and other medical institutions around the world. Leprosariums bring restored hope and health to thousands in the countries where leprosy is rampant.

Forty-eight hundred elementary schools, 416 high schools and colleges, and two universities train thousands of Christian youth on six continents. In these institutions of learning emphasis is on the development of the head, the hand, and the heart. Boys and girls, young men and young women, are prepared to live for Christ in this present world and to live *with* Him in the world to come.

The work of the church is no "pie in the sky" program. As certain as there is a heaven to win and a hell to shun, just so sure there is a work to be done here and now. The body, mind, and soul of man challenge the follower of Christ in this present world. To do their part in meeting this challenge is the work and the ministry to which Seventh-day Adventists are dedicated.

*Friday*

# A Family With a Heart

On July 26, 1963, a devastating earthquake in Skoplje, Yugoslavia, left thousands of people homeless. In the city at the time was a Seventh-day Adventist church with about two hundred members. Eighty-five of these members lost everything they possessed. When their Adventist brethren in Denmark heard of the disaster, they went to work. Not only did they send a sizable contribution to help relieve the suffering in general in Skoplje, but they determined to do something special for their fellow Adventists in the stricken area.

Quickly funds were raised for the purchase of twelve prefab houses with beds, tables, chairs, heaters, stoves, and kitchen equipment for each home. They shipped this tangible evidence of their concern and love by train to Yugoslavia. But this was not all. A carload of men from Denmark drove to Skoplje and personally participated in the erection and furnishing of the new homes.

The people in Skoplje did not understand the Danish language, but they understood the language of love that led their Adventist friends in Denmark to expend time, effort, and money to be helpful in time of disaster.

Seventh-day Adventists by no means confine their help to members of their own communion. In fact, only a very small percentage of their activities are so directed. Our horizons include all who may be in need. Paul reminds us that "pure religion and undefiled before God and the Father is this, To visit the fatherless and widows in their affliction, and to keep himself unspotted from the world." (James 1:27.)

The church operates 2,694 welfare units and centers which, with other agencies operating in 190 countries, gave help to more than eight million people in 1967. Food and clothing valued at over 26 million dollars were distributed to the needy.

When an earthquake in Iran left thousands homeless, injured, or dead, a Seventh-day Adventist missionary was one of the first to reach the outside world via his ham radio. Within minutes he was in touch with headquarters of the church in Washington, D.C. Word flashed back, "One hundred thirty bales of clothing, $17,000 worth of penicillin and vitamins shipped and cash available." This was only a beginning, for the church decided to rebuild an entire village that had been destroyed. Some weeks later with American and Iranian officials present the disaster victims were admitted to their new brick village.

In Texas a hurricane took scores of lives and left

thousands homeless. Seventh-day Adventist state welfare workers were on the job within hours. Hundreds were fed and clothed. A Baptist man had lost his home. Seventh-day Adventists moved in and built an entirely new three-bedroom house for him in just one day. Work began at daybreak. By midafternoon the painting was finished, the gas, light, water, and telephone were installed. By sunset the furniture was in and flowers were in the planter, and the family had a new home to replace the one they had lost just a short time before.

And so it goes—when earthquakes shook Peru, Turkey, Iran; when hurricanes laid waste large areas of Mexico or islands of the West Indies; when tornadoes struck in Kansas, Texas, or Louisiana, Seventh-day Adventists moved in with help and healing. "Wherever there is a naked body, an empty stomach, or a broken heart, there lies the challenge to the church."

Wherever there are disasters—war, fires, floods, earthquakes, or tornadoes—Adventists do their best to help.

"Inasmuch as ye have done it unto one of the least of these my brethren," Jesus said, "ye have done it unto me." Matthew 25:40. Christians who care will minister to their Lord through the needs of those about them. Caring for others is one of the most important signs of true Christianity.

*Saturday*

# Christianity Removes Barriers

"For ye are all the children of God by faith in Christ Jesus. For as many of you as have been baptized into Christ have put on Christ. There is neither Jew nor Greek, there is neither bond nor free, there is neither male nor female: for ye are all one in Christ Jesus." Galatians 3:26-28.

We live today in a world separated by nationalism, ablaze with racism, riven with tribal hatred and suspicions. I have witnessed it in the countries of Africa; and many of us have seen it or read about it in the cities of America, in Vietnam, and in the Middle East. Ethnic and national differences all too frequently breed suspicion and hatred, resulting in bloodshed and devastation.

If Jesus were here in person today, He would say, as He did to Peter two thousand years ago, "Put up again thy sword." Matthew 26:52. The Christian shuns violence.

Seventh-day Adventists are not nationalists. We are not an American church, nor a European, nor an Asian, nor an African church. We are part of a great worldwide family and fellowship. In this family with a mission "to every nation, and kindred, and tongue, and people" (Revelation 14:6) we are "neither Jew nor Greek"; we are rather "all one in Christ Jesus" (Galatians 3:28).

There is no room for narrow nationalism or racism in God's family. When Christ died on the cross two millenniums ago, He abolished forever any separating barriers. As Paul says, the Saviour "has broken down the dividing wall of hostility." (Ephesians 2:14, R.S.V.) He has "abolished in His flesh the enmity" that might ideologically or naturally exist between governments or races.

In Christ the old hatreds are banished; a mutual love for Him binds hearts together in Christian affection and fellowship. We are indeed "one in Christ Jesus."

*Sunday*

# Serving God Is Not Always Easy

Maria was attending religious meetings in a small Central American country. Night after night she listened intently as the gospel of the kingdom was proclaimed by a dedicated lay preacher. Like winged arrows the shafts of truth sank deep into her heart. She decided there was but one thing to do— she must follow Christ and prepare for baptism.

When Maria told her husband of her conviction and plans, he was furious.

"If you are baptized into that church," he shouted, "I will kill you!"

Maria had a difficult decision to make. To follow the dictates of her conscience might cost her life. But she finally decided to join the church and trust her future to God's care, and she was baptized.

When Maria returned from the baptism that Sabbath, her husband was waiting for her at the front door. He was sharpening a nasty-looking machete.

"Didn't I tell you I would kill you if you were baptized?" he shrilled.

"Yes, dear," Maria replied quietly, "you told me, and I am ready. I have made everything right with God, and I am ready to die!"

The husband's jaw dropped. His knife almost slipped from his hand. "You really mean that?" he stammered in unbelief. "Well, if that church can give you such faith and courage, I am going to join, too." Today Maria and her husband are united in their church fellowship and in their determination to be ready when Jesus comes.

But all such stories do not have happy endings. Helena's father threatened to shoot her if she insisted on being baptized. The day of her baptism the enraged father followed his daughter to the river where the service was to be held. He had a rifle in his hand.

When her turn came, Helena walked into the water and the pastor lifted his arm and began speaking. "My dear sister, upon your profession of faith in the Lord Jesus Christ and His power to save you from sin, I now baptize you——"

A shot rang out. Helena collapsed in the water. Another shot, and the pastor fell. By the time friends reached her Helena was dead. The pastor was badly wounded but recovered. Another youthful Christian had surrendered her life for her Lord. In prison a repentant father also found his Saviour and, months later, followed his daughter down into the waters of baptism.

"Be thou faithful unto death," Christ promised, "and I will give thee a crown of life." Revelation 2:10.

Yes, sometimes the cost of joining God's family is high, but despite the price, thousands are taking the step.

*Monday*

# A Family Reunion Soon

In December, 1966, we had a family reunion at our home in Washington, D.C. For the first time both of our sons and their families were all with us. It was a blessed experience to be together. Mrs. Pier-

Christ does not force Himself on man—He knocks
at the mind's door, waiting to be invited in.

son and I had looked forward to and planned for this day. How wonderful to have all the children and all of the grandchildren with us!

There is another family reunion scheduled for the very near future. This will be at the second coming of Jesus when the family of earth becomes the family of heaven.

In the fourteenth chapter of John, Jesus makes it very clear that He is loath to be separated from His loved ones. He longs to have His earthbound children with Him in that heavenly home which He has gone to prepare for those who love Him.

"I go to prepare a place for you," He says in accents tender, "and if I go and prepare a place for you, I will come again, and receive you unto myself; that where I am, there ye may be also." John 14:2, 3.

What a glorious day that will be—all the family of God together, never to part! No more partings, no more sad good-byes, no more long separations, for God's loved ones will be together for eternity. What a privilege to be numbered with the redeemed when the saints go marching home! The Apostle Paul says, "The whole creation is on tiptoe to see the wonderful sight of the sons of God coming into their own." Romans 8:19, Phillips.

By God's grace and with His help, I am determined to be among God's redeemed ones on that glorious day! If we plan to be part of the family of God in heaven, we must be part of the family of God on earth. The Saviour extends to each of us a loving invitation to become part of that great family today.

"Behold, I stand at the door, and knock: if any man hear my voice, and open the door, I will come in to him, and will sup with him, and he with me." Revelation 3:20.

Will *you* let Him in just now?

# INDEX